Semper Fi

The Story of a Vietnam Era Marine

Orville Leverne Clubb

SEMPER FI gives a portrait of a young man and his experiences as an enlisted member of the US Marine Corps during the Vietnam War. Orville Clubb begins at the beginning with his earliest memories and tells the story right through to his discharge after serving overseas. Born into a poor family brought together by World War II, the writer grew to maturity as a young marine. As with many young men of this era of similar socioeconomic status, joining the military as an enlisted man was an attractive option that offered a new start in life.

DR. ORVILLE LEVERNE CLUBB was born on 18 June 1944, in Pascagoula, Mississippi. He attended public schools in both Mississippi and Los Angeles, California, graduating from Garfield High School, Los Angeles, in 1962. He then spent more than four years as an enlisted man in the US Marines achieving the rank of sergeant (E5) prior to being released from active duty in late 1966. As a civilian, he started in the Information Communications Technology field in late 1966 at the Bank of America in Los Angeles and then at the Bank of Hawai'i in Honolulu. In August 1977, Dr. Clubb moved to Hong Kong as a senior lecturer at the Hong Kong Polytechnic. In the 1970s up to his retirement in 2009, Dr. Clubb held many posts in Southeast Asia, in both academia and the computer industry. In higher education, he has been Dean of an engineering and technology faculty, Acting Dean of a business faculty, Associate Principal of a large college, Head of an academic division, and an Associate Head of an academic department. In industry he has worked mostly in banking but was the Systems Support Manager for Burroughs (HK) in the 1980s. Dr. Clubb holds a BA degree in Psychology from the University of Hawai'i, a Diploma in Chinese Law from the University of East Asia, Macau (now the University of Macau) and a PhD in Computing from The University of Sunderland in the UK. Now retired, he commutes between Hong Kong and Hawai'i, where he has a macadamia nut and coffee farm.

Semper Fi

The Story of a Vietnam Era Marine

Orville Leverne Clubb

Proverse Hong Kong

Semper Fi: The Story of a Vietnam Era Marine
by Orville Leverne Clubb.
2nd Edition pbk published in Hong Kong by Proverse Hong Kong, February 2016.
ISBN: 978-988-8228-21-8
Copyright © Proverse Hong Kong, February 2016.

1st published in pbk in Hong Kong by Proverse Hong Kong, 23 March 2012.
ISBN 978-988-19933-4-2
Copyright © Proverse Hong Kong, 23 March 2012.

1st pbk edition distribution
(Hong Kong and worldwide):
Chinese University Press of Hong Kong, Chinese University of Hong Kong, Shatin, NT, Hong Kong SAR.
E-mail: cup-bus@cuhk.edu.hk Web site: www.chineseupress.com
(United Kingdom)
Christine Penney, Stratford-upon-Avon, Warwickshire CV37 6DN, England. Email: <chrisp@proversepublishing.com>

Enquiries: Proverse Hong Kong, P. O. Box 259, Tung Chung Post Office, Tung Chung, Lantau Island, NT, Hong Kong SAR, China.
E-mail: proverse@netvigator.com Web site: www.proversepublishing.com

The right of Orville Leverne Clubb to be identified as the author of this work has been asserted by him in accordance with the Copyright, Designs and Patents Act 1988.
Cover photograph supplied by and © Orville Leverne Clubb.
Cover design by Artist Hong Kong Company.

All rights reserved. No part of this publication may be reproduced, stored in a retrieval system, or transmitted, in any form or by any means, electronic, mechanical, photocopying, recording or otherwise, without the prior written permission of the publisher. The book is sold subject to the condition that it shall not, by way of trade or otherwise, be lent, re-sold, hired out or otherwise circulated without the publisher's prior written consent in any form of binding or cover other than that in which it is published and without a similar condition including this condition being imposed on the subsequent owner or purchaser. Please contact Proverse Hong Kong in writing, to request any and all permissions (including but not restricted to republishing, inclusion in anthologies, translation, reading, performance
and use as set pieces in examinations and festivals).

Proverse Hong Kong

1st pbk ed. British Library Cataloguing in Publication Data

Clubb, Orville Leverne, 1944-
Semper Fi : the story of a Vietnam era Marine.
1. Clubb, Orville Leverne, 1944- 2. Marines--United States--Biography. 3. Vietnam War, 1961-1975--Personal narratives, American. 4. United States. Marine Corps. Marines, 5th. Battalion, 3rd.--History. 5. Vietnam War, 1961-1975--Veterans--United States--Biography.
I. Title
359.9'6'092-dc23

ISBN-13: 9789881993342

PREFACE

As a British ex-soldier who fought in the deserts of North Africa and later in Italy, who in World War Two was Mentioned in Dispatches, and with German shrapnel still in my body, it is natural I was eager to read *Semper Fi* (always faithful). This chronicles the experiences of an American Marine, one of the "Honoured Brotherhood", during the unpopular Vietnam War. Incidentally, the Vietnamese call it "The American War".

Basic training must be similar for soldiers in countries the world over. Recruits are humiliated in uncouth language with no regard for feelings or self-esteem. The secret is for the recruit to accept the insults like "water off a duck's back", while the instructors' aim is to recruit "boys" and, after three months basic training, to turn them out as "men".

Once in action a soldier soon realises that, if a shell comes over with his number on it, there is little he can do about it. He believes in fate. In war, if a young man has to die, it is appropriate he falls in combat. One very positive thing I remember from World War Two was the *camaraderie*. You could generally rely on stout fellows in your own unit when you found yourself in a "tight corner". The author implies a similar spirit existed in Vietnam.

This interesting book includes a considerable amount of preliminary detail. For "short-arm inspections", "other ranks" lined up and underwent a cursory examination by a medical officer for "clap". It was not a crime to contract venereal disease but it was a crime not to report it.

Eventually, the "Warriors of the Brotherhood" who had managed to survive returned to their native land. From the Allies' viewpoint, most people considered World War Two was a just war. We Britons returned home to what could be described as "a heroes' welcome". That was not the case with military personnel returning to America after service in what had been Indo-China.

The United States was a "divided country". Many Americans felt their interference in Vietnam was unjust and unnecessary. The author and other returning military personnel were not welcomed home as heroes. Indeed the United States later "lost face" by withdrawing all their troops from Vietnam.

At first the author did not relish talking about the carnage and his Vietnam "experiences". Later, he "opened up". It was the same after the Second World War. If you could discuss it, it was helpful, getting war experiences "out of your system".

The author has written *Semper Fi* because he wanted to clear the "misunderstandings" which existed in America about the Vietnam War. How successful he has been is up to you, the reader, to judge.

Dr Dan Waters ISO, BBS
British World War Two Soldier

Contents

Preface by Dan Waters, ISO, BBS, PhD	v
Prologue	1
1 Early Days	2
2 Jackson and Biloxi	10
3 Back to Gulfport	14
4 California	22
5 Back to Grandma's House	26
6 Montebello	31
7 Back to East Los Angeles	35
8 Garfield Days	39
9 Leaving Home for Marine Corps Boot Camp	48
10 Starting Boot Camp	57
11 Camp Matthews and Marksmanship Training	65
12 MCRD after Marksmanship Training	72
13 Infantry Training Regiment	77
14 Home Leave and the Missiles of October 1962	83
15 Electronics School MCRD	87
16 Posting to 1st Marine Division	91
17 Sub Unit #1, 1st Marine Division	99
18 Forming 3/5 from Sub Unit #1	105
19 Transport Ship to Okinawa	109
20 Okinawa	113
21 Okinawa to Subic Bay	118
22 Operation Hilltop and Jungle Survival Training	124
23 Final Days Prior to Deckhouse 1	129
24 Deckhouse 1	133
25 Operation Nathan Hale	142
26 Back to Subic Bay and Olongapo	145
27 Deckhouse 2	152
28 Operation Hastings	155
29 Deactivation of BLT 3/5 and Operation Colorado	163
30 Getting Ready to Muster Out	168
31 Going Stateside	173
32 Home at Last	177

Epilogue 180
Early Responses to *Semper Fi*
– By Alan J. Zygowicz, Major USMC, Special Agent in 187
Charge, Hong Kong Office, US Secret Service 1996-1999.
– By Kelley Douglas, MD, PhD. 188
Glossary 189

Permissions and Sources for Illustrations

Images 1, 2, 3, 4 and 5 were taken with the Clubb family camera. Images 6, 7, 8, and 9 are from the Author's personal collection. Image 10 is in the public domain because it contains materials that originally came from the United States Marine Corps. [*Source:*
http://upload.wikimedia.org/wikipedia/commons/7/7d/Dong_Ha%2C_Vietnam_Operation_Hastings.jpg]
Image 11 is adapted by the Author from http://www.popasmoke.com/visions/images/image_1886.jpg. Acknowledgement is made to Visions – Photo Archive, USMC/COMBAT HELICOPTER ASSOCIATION.

Illustrations
(between pp. 71 and 72)

Author's mother and father with himself as a baby, Pascagoula, 1944.   a

In front of the house on Searle Avenue, 1951.   b
From left: Author's grandmother, the Author as a boy, Author's grandfather ("Papa"), Sergeant Tosh.

In front of the apartment building in Montebello, Easter 1954. Left to right: front row, Author's siblings, Sandy, Sue and Doug; back row, Author's father, Author, Author's mother and Author's sister, Kitty.   b

Mr. Empt and Author as a boy outside Mr Empt's house, 1948.   c

Author and siblings after a family trip to Tijuana, August 1953. In front of the East Los Angeles house that burned down. Front: Doug. From left to right: 2nd row: Kitty and Sandy. 3rd row: Sue and Author.   c

Platoon 144, September 1962. Front row: from left to right: Drill instructors Corporal Miller, Staff Sergeant Drake, Sergeant Yoder and Sergeant Smallwood; Back row (*centre*), Private Orville L. Clubb.   d

Northern Training area, Okinawa. Swimming hole, May 1966.   d

Boot Camp, graduation picture, 1962.   e

Northern Training area, Okinawa, May 1966.   e

Operation Hastings, 15 July-3 August 1966. Marines of Company H, 2nd Battalion, 4th Marine Regiment, take to the water, as they move to join up with other elements of their battalion. Photographer, Unknown USMC marine.   f

Operation Hastings sketch-map.   f

PROLOGUE

Very few people realize that the Vietnam War was the most costly war the US Marine Corps has ever fought. During the Vietnam War, five times as many marines died in combat as in World War I, three times as many as in Korea, and more were killed and wounded than in all of World War II. The Corps fought true to our adopted name, Devil Dogs, given to us by the Germans in World War I. The Corps never lost a major battle during the Vietnam War.

As a veteran of this unpopular war I was surprised at the reception I received on returning home. Time is healing this resentment and now many people ask: "How was it?" As do the majority of veterans, I feel that most people do not have an experience base to understand what we went through even if they were told. I normally greet such a question with silence.

Seeing several websites dedicated to veterans of the Vietnam War and my fighting unit, 3rd Battalion 5th Marines (3/5) I realize that my cohort of veterans is passing away very fast. We are rapidly losing the history of this war. Because of this, I thought that I should tell my story and the story of Battalion Landing Team 3/5 since many of my memories will also be lost with my death.

The young men whom I served with were mostly recent civilians barely out of high school who had been called upon by our government to spend time in hell. These young marines held the power of life or death and faced this heavy responsibility with dignity and coolness, often having to make a lethal decision in a split second. The young marines I served with were the finest group of young men I have ever been around. We were a family that loved each other more than our biological families. As the US Marines' motto, *Semper Fidelis (Semper Fi)* implies, we were always faithful – to our government and the Marine Corps, and ultimately to ourselves.

CHAPTER ONE

EARLY DAYS

MY early memories are fading, and as my degree in psychology taught me, we all get false memories of the past as we age. Human memories are not images recorded by a camcorder that leave us a movie of our past, but are a system of memories that is greatly influenced by emotions, our past experiences, what we want to believe, what we are told and our new experiences. We modify our memories of the past to fit into our memory system to enable us to keep our sanity. Therefore, memories are not necessarily the truth but the truth as each of us sees it. I thought that I should document some of my memory of the Vietnam War "as I see it" for my children and my brothers who were marines serving with me, while I can.

You may wonder what kind of background would cause a young man to enlist in to the United States Marine Corps in the early 1960s. While I was in the Corps on active duty I met people from all over the US and from other countries. The military is a caste system consisting of two major castes: the enlisted and officer grades. The Corps is no different, if anything the castes are stronger since it is a naval service. In the enlisted ranks in the 1960s, we tended to be mostly from the lower socioeconomic strata of society. The Corps offers a young man the chance to grow physically and mentally and gives him a sense of belonging to a much-honored brotherhood. There is feeling of pride and prestige in saying "I am a marine" or "I am a former marine." The attraction is the same as offered by street gangs: a group of people that stand up for each other and a sense of belonging. I cannot speak for others, but I will start this story with my background.

I was born on 18 June 1944, at Jackson County Hospital in Pascagoula, Mississippi, as a nine-and-a-half-pound, two-month premature baby. In later life, I questioned my mom about the fact that I was born only seven months after her wedding day. To her embarrassment, she admitted that she was two months pregnant when she married my dad. My dad was a US sailor and my mom and grandmother were welders at Ingalls Shipbuilding Corporation in Pascagoula during World War II. My mom and dad met when the US Navy sent my dad as part of a crew to ferry a new ship from the shipyard around to the East Coast of the US. I guess many of my generation would have had a similar start. Wars have caused many a hasty marriage. Perhaps war is a way of getting diversity in the human gene pool since families tend to stay in the same geographical area of their youth. War causes people to travel and mingle with others.

I had the misfortune of being given the nickname of Junior. I understand that Mom and Dad used to joke about "when Junior is born" and that name stuck! My earliest memories are of a house in Gulfport, Mississippi, at 2302 Searle Avenue, with my extended family, which included my uncle Sam, who was still a teenager, my mother (who was also a teenager), my grandfather, whom I called "Papa," and grandmother. However, we were minus my dad. To me, this house was heaven; it proved to be my sanctuary over the early years of my life.

Our house was situated on three acres of land just a little over one block north of the railroad tracks and East Railroad Street. If you went south and crossed the tracks going toward Highway 90 and the Gulf of Mexico, you entered a totally different world. The homes across the tracks were much nicer. As a child, I never understood the meaning of the saying "he came from the wrong side of the tracks." Now I realize that as you moved north from Highway 90, the people were poorer until you got to what we politically correctly called in those days, the colored quarters where the poorest lived. We were situated between the fine mansions of the rich with a view of the Gulf and the middle class who lived on 2nd Street on one side, and the colored quarters on the other. Looking back, this tells us quite a lot about our socioeconomic status. Even though we were poor, Papa had recovered fairly well considering that he had lost his land during the Depression and had had to work as a sharecropper for a number of years. He had recovered enough to buy this new house and parcel of land.

The area that the house was situated on was carved out of woods. Behind and to the sides of the house the land was still wild. The house fronted on Searle Avenue, which was a dirt road, and we were very close to the junction of Searle Avenue and 23rd Street. In those days, 23rd Street ended at Searle Avenue. We did not have a car so we relied on public transportation. To catch the city bus you would walk from the house down 23rd Street, which was also a dirt road, one long block away to Hewes Avenue, which was a paved main road and where the city bus stop was. Once on the bus, you could go downtown to Gulfport. In my youth, the buses had a sign in the middle of the sitting area dividing the buses into two separate sections – namely, the back area of the bus for coloreds; and the front seats for whites.

The educational standard of my family was low. My mother had reached the eleventh grade before giving up on her education. My uncle Sam was in high school at the time we moved to the new house and I believe that he finished. My father had a third-grade education and I'm not sure about Grandma and Papa. I know that when Grandma wrote letters to me after I left Gulfport, she would never punctuate her writing making it difficult to read. Papa was a voracious reader of the Bible and books on religion, but his handwriting was virtually unreadable.

When Dad returned from the war, we all lived with my grandparents for a while. My dad was a restless man and had a very unsettled nature about him. I know very little about his side of the family since we always lived near and associated with my mother's family. According to my mother, he was a handsome man; he stood 5 feet 10 inches tall and had black hair and green-brown eyes. He was from Poplar Bluff, Missouri, and was raised on a farm. My dad told me that after he had joined the US Navy he spent time as a gunner's mate on a ship named the USS *Scott*. During his tour on the *Scott*, he took part in a transport mission to take goods to Russia. The *Scott* was assigned escort duty for a convoy of merchant ships. Many years later, I found from the Web that the USS *Scott* was a destroyer escort, commissioned on 20 July 1943. The U-boats had missed his ship but had picked off a number of other ships in his convoy. I learned from Dad's sister, Aunt Freda, that Dad's father, my grandfather, was shot dead in front of my dad on the family's front porch in Poplar Bluff when Dad was ten years old. There was a rumor from my grandmother that Grandfather Clubb had taken part in a bank robbery during the Depression and it was the local sheriff who had shot him in the back. It is hard to judge the veracity of the story since Dad and Grandma had their own mutual hate society. Also, I remember that Dad used to have "sleep-walking" fits, when he would get up and start running in his sleep. He would jump through the glass in windows and run into doors before he would wake. He had been to the Department of Veterans Affairs (VA) on many occasions but they could not diagnose the cause. Mom told me that she thought the cause was that Dad and some of his shipmates had thrown a fellow shipmate overboard at sea. This may have been a confession Dad made to Mom, but she did not want to say she knew for sure. Whatever the cause, Dad had a demon that would occasionally take control during his sleep.

I remember walking in the woods at the back of the house with Dad when we spotted a couple of squirrels playing. Squirrels are considered game in the South and have a nice taste similar to chicken – I'm told that in the Depression, most of the meat on the table came from hunting and anything that moved could be killed, cooked and eaten. The two squirrels panicked when they realized that we were close. We saw them go into a hole in a small hollow tree trying to hide from us. Dad examined the tree and noted that there was a hole a little way up that he could block to prevent the two squirrels from escaping. There was also a smaller hole about waist high to Dad where the hollowing of the tree began. He inserted a piece of wood in the top hole to seal it and took out two cigarettes and tore off the cigarette paper. He then took some green leaves and built a fire in the bottom hole of the tree with the tobacco and green leaves. What he wanted was just smoke, because the squirrels would not come out of the hole if there were flames at the bottom hole. As the smoke built up inside the hollow tree, you could hear the squirrels racing around inside looking for a way out. In desperation, one finally came out of the bottom hole where Dad was waiting with another piece of wood, a heavy branch off a dead tree he had found nearby. As the first squirrel exited the tree, he hit it directly on the top of its head, killing it instantly. The second squirrel held out for a while, but finally gave in to the smoke and met his grief in a similar fashion trying to escape through the bottom hole. We took the two squirrels home, where Grandma chicken-fried them for supper. Kentucky Fried Chicken has nothing on the recipe that Grandma had for chicken-frying meat.

~~

In 1947, Gulfport was hit by a terrible hurricane. I have only a spotty memory of the hurricane and its aftermath, but I do remember that there was a tidal surge that damaged a lot of the very nice mansions along Highway 90. At the time, there was only a seawall alongside the highway and the tidal surge had jumped the seawall, crossed the highway and had gotten all the way to many of the fine homes along the waterfront causing a lot of damage. That same year, my mother gave birth to my sister Lois and my uncle Sam married my aunt Sid, whose maiden name was Sadie Burke. Also in 1947, Mom and Dad decided to start a new life and set out on their own with their new baby Sue (Lois's nickname) leaving me with my grandparents. On her deathbed, my mom told me that she did not abandon me back at the tender age of three, but she could not take me away from my grandmother since Grandma loved me so much. Whatever the reason, I was left to live with my grandparents in Gulfport, Mississippi. My parents moved to Jackson, Mississippi.

Papa worked at the VA hospital in Gulfport as a nurse's aid. He had the 2:00 pm to midnight shift and would leave to walk to work every day in the early afternoon in his hospital uniform and his hat. The VA hospital was around half a mile away from home. In the spring or summer, I would wake up to find Papa working his garden in his work clothes and his hat. Papa wore a hat at all times when he was outside. Grandma was an expert at canning and preserving all types of food, so we were provided for year round from Papa's garden. Papa was a tall man for a person born in the 1800s. He was 6 feet 3 inches tall with jet black hair and had inherited many of the facial features of his part Native American ancestry. He had steely blue eyes that were very gentle. He had that rare mixture of strength and gentleness. When he finished a chore, he would always say "thank the Lord." Whenever someone did something for him, he would say "much obliged." He always tipped his hat at people. All in all, the Papa of my memories, a man whom I knew and loved, was a first class God-fearing Southern gentleman.

My food as a child was described as "soul food" in California. We had black-eyed peas and cornbread, fresh tomatoes, ribs, mustard greens and, to the surprise of many Asians, rice. Grandma would never waste food; if we had leftovers it appeared at the next meal as a different dish. One of my favorites was Sloppy Joe sandwiches. The filler of Sloppy Joes was made up of leftovers that were enhanced with ground beef and chili powder. Also, what we called dinner was normally the noon meal, and we would have a light "supper" prior to going to bed.

We had a chicken coop and for a while a pig pen on the property. The chickens provided us with eggs and an occasional chicken dinner. This extra source of food supplemented our meals. Grandma had a great technique for killing chickens; she would grab the chicken by its head and swing it around a couple of times and with a wrist action, snap off its head. The chicken would run around the yard for a while before dying. I guess this is where the phrase "running around like a chicken with its head cut off" came from. At times, there were battles between snakes and Grandma over the eggs. Since we lived near the woods, an occasional snake would decide that the eggs in Grandma's chicken coop were an easy target. Grandma was ruthless when she found a snake near the coop. I guess it was a competition for the next meal between the family and the snake.

When Papa kept pigs, they were at the far corner of the property and downwind to keep the smell from the house. Even though I was very young, I still remember very vividly Papa slaughtering one of our hogs. One day there was a lot of commotion at the pig pen so I went to investigate. To my horror, I arrived in time to see Papa slaughter one of our hogs with an axe. As he hit the hog on the head with the blunt end of the axe's head, the hog let go of all its bodily functions and dropped to its knees on its front legs, at which point Papa gave the killing blow to the neck with the sharp side of the axe's head. The pig was dressed out and put into a large container of boiling water to remove its hair. The pig provided us with meat for a long time.

As I mentioned earlier, Papa was a pious man; religion to him was an obsession. Every Sunday we would dress up and go to Sister Lee's Pentecostal Church where Papa was a Sunday school teacher. The church was located a ways away from the house and required a bus ride to get there. It was a small church that could seat about thirty to fifty people. Behind the altar, the church had a large deep baptismal pool. It was a walk-in pool where people being baptized could be completely immersed in water. I remember that Holy Communion was given with a set of very small glasses, much smaller than shot glasses, containing grape juice and cut-up white bread. When I questioned why there was no wine, I was told that in the Bible the reference to wine really meant grape juice or unfermented wine. The service was always a joyous occasion with hymns and a fiery sermon given by Sister Lee. If the members of the congregation approved of the sermon they would give an "amen" or a "praise the Lord." Church in the South is a passion that has to be emotionally felt.

Papa's religion was one that kept him from drinking any alcohol, coffee or other stimulant (tea was okay). We did not have a television since the "box" was the "devil's tool." We had a radio but that was only for news and the radio ministry. Initially, I was not allowed to watch movies. An occasional bit of entertainment was when a tent revival would come through town and the poor sinners of Gulfport that had "backslid" would have the chance "to be born again." Some of the tent revivals had healers who dealt with the sick and afflicted. These revivals would work up to a feverish pitch, with music and speaking in tongues. I am sure the raw emotion of a tent revival cannot be duplicated today with a modern rave party.

Life with Grandma and Papa was one of a lot of love and much discipline. However, Papa was never one to be the disciplinarian; to me he was kind and always seemed to be in good spirits. Grandma was always very much in control. She used a tool of punishment called a "switch." A switch is a small thin branch of a tree, preferably a peach tree branch. If used properly, a switch can draw blood. The beating would be administered to the naked upper part of the legs since we normally wore shorts. Corporal punishment with a switch would leave a long memory of what you had done wrong. I remember one time in the 1950s I was told to be home by 7:00 pm when I was taken to the movies by our neighbor Marisa Empt. Marisa wanted to see the coronation of Queen Elizabeth II that was showing in the movie house in Gulfport and took me along. When I arrived home at 8:00 pm, after watching a ceremony that I could not understand as a young kid and found boring, Grandma was waiting with her switch. The beating must have been effective; to this day if I'm about to be late, I get very anxious.

In 1948, when I was four years old, my cousin Kelley was born to Uncle Sam and Aunt Sid. In 1949, Papa sold Uncle Sam a one-acre plot of land from his three acres. The plot was also on

Searle Avenue. That same year, my sister Sandy was born in Jackson.

At that time, Uncle Sam was a professional musician with his own band and played at various clubs along the Gulf Coast. Uncle Sam and Aunt Sid cleared the plot of land with the occasional help of Papa. It was a nice family project and an attempt was made to make the hollow tiles needed for the construction with a hollow tile mold. I do not know where the plan had come from but I do remember the translucent glass-brick tile skylight that was built into the curve of the house on its southwestern face. The skylight was to act like a window and let daylight in to the living room, but since it was glass brick and translucent, not transparent, it provided privacy.

Family life with my grandparents was a good time of Southern summers spent playing in the dirt road in front of the house and going to neighbors' houses to sneak a look at this great new invention called television, which Papa would not have. I had no fears or worries – life was well taken care of.

CHAPTER TWO

JACKSON AND BILOXI

THE year 1950 was very eventful for the family. My brother Doug was born; Aunt Sid and Uncle Sam had their second child, my cousin Steven; and late in the year, my own life changed drastically. In September, I had started school in the first grade for the 1950/1951 school year at Northeast Elementary School, and needed to get up every morning to go to class. However, also in 1950, Papa bought a bakery/restaurant in Biloxi. I was six years old and the family decided that it was time that I returned to my mom and dad who now lived in Jackson, Mississippi. Everyone figured that Papa and Grandma would be busy with the new business venture and looking after a six-year-old was an additional burden. I changed to a school in Jackson and continued the first grade.

Jackson was quite a dramatic change. I went from being the only child being looked after and pampered by Grandma and Papa to being the oldest of a family of four. Not only was it a family of four, but a family with two very young babies – so there was little attention given to me. Dad was working as a welder and Mom was a stay-home mom and took care of the family. I have very sketchy memories of the time in Jackson. I know that I was not adapting well to the family. Perhaps we forget the unpleasant things as we grow older. The major good thing that I remember is Grandma and Papa had bought me a brand new bicycle for Christmas, which was delivered to Jackson. I was the apple of Grandma's eye, which caused much understandable jealousy in other members of the family; Grandma would always give me the best she could afford but not treat the other grandkids in the same pampered way. I had taken over from Uncle Sam as the baby of the family since he was now grown.

I do not remember much about school in Jackson except that we were required to have an afternoon nap and I, at times, pretended to be asleep since I usually felt active and did not want to rest. I had made pretending an art, and I remember testing my skill at pretending by "oversleeping." The teacher would not force kids to go back to their seats till they woke up. After the teacher had called the class to their seats and enough time had passed, I faked a wakeup and went to my seat and gave an extra big yawn.

I remember Mom making cupcakes and I would go around to the industrial shops that were close by our house to sell them. Dad was talking about making a little metal display carry-case for me from which to sell the cakes, as I was doing so well with them and was then taking them around in a cardboard box.

Dad had found religion for a while, and to me, for a change, he seemed to be reasonable. I remember Dad asking Mom to go to church one evening and Mom refusing, saying that she had been forced to go to church as a kid and hated it. That evening, Dad and I went together to one of Jackson's black churches. They let Dad play the bass in the church band; he loved to play gospel music. Later, I knew that Dad had "backslid" when one day I saw him smoking his beloved cigars and dipping snuff again. This was sad, since religion kept Dad in check and made him far more settled. If Mom had embraced religion again in Jackson, family life could have had a very different outcome.

The family of my mom's brother Buster and Uncle Sam's family were in Jackson at the same time as Dad and Mom. Uncle Sam had moved up from Gulfport and his band was playing at a local Jackson night-club. My uncle Buster was a man with a mean streak. I found him very unlike my uncle Sam, who was always like an older brother to me and had a gentle nature. Uncle Buster had two daughters, Mary who was one year older than me and Linda who was one year younger. I do not know why, but one afternoon in front of Uncle Buster's place, he wanted Mary and Linda to fight me. The two girls were set on me as if they were his two hunting dogs and I was his game. I was able to get Mary to cry very quickly but my cousin Linda was a very spirited young girl and finally got the best of me, sending me home crying, which greatly amused my uncle Buster. When Dad learned this, he told me that if I ever lost a fight again I would get a beating when I got home.

A very vivid memory from my short time in Jackson was when I had my tonsils taken out and was at the same time circumcised. I remember that I could have all the ice cream that I wanted, but would throw it up. Dad was visiting me and I had to throw up and he put out his cigarette in the tray after I vomited up blood. I hated cigarettes, so this I found disgusting. The circumcision caused pain for a few days and required Vaseline to be put on the wound till it healed.

Dad kept rabbits in the back of the house. One day one of my cousins let a rabbit out of its hutch in our backyard. Dad came home early that evening and learned that the rabbit had escaped, and I was instantly blamed. I remember that Dad was yelling at me and I kept trying to tell him I did not do it. He threw me to the ground in the backyard, took off his belt and started to beat me. It seemed as if he would never stop. The pain of the belt on my flesh was near to unbearable. I curled up in the fetal position trying to make my body as small as possible as the belting continued. It was as if Dad was taking out all his frustration of a lifetime on me. Perhaps it was because I was the reason he had had to marry and give up his freedom or because I had lost the fight with my girl cousins or I was not the son that he wanted. The beating seemed to go on for an eternity. This was the most painful thing I had ever experienced either physically or emotionally in my life; the belt was far more painful than Grandma's switches. When he finally stopped, I had welts and bruises all over my back and my legs. Mom was not at home at the time. When she returned and saw what had happened, she told me to pack my things and that she was sending me back to live with Papa and Grandma.

Grandma arranged to have one of our neighbors drive her up to Jackson to take me back to Gulfport. I remember with mixed feelings getting in the car. The thing that stands out most about that trip back to Gulfport is that Grandma had packed a lunch of her Southern fried chicken. There was no one who could cook chicken the way that Grandma could and the familiar taste of the chicken was very comforting. I moved in with Papa and Grandma to a room in the back of their bakery shop in Biloxi and started at my third school for first grade. Papa and Grandma had kept their house in Gulfport but did not want to commute since Papa did not own or drive a car and the bakery was taking up too much time. I will never forget the taste of fresh, glazed, still-warm doughnuts, like manna from heaven. To this day, I've never tasted doughnuts like the fresh ones Papa made.

Life in the bakery was good to me but was taking a toll on Papa. He would get up at 3:30 am and start baking for the day, and would close in the evening around 7:00 pm. It would then take to 9:30 pm to clean up and do the accounts for the day. This was his daily routine; Papa had become a slave to the bakery. The new business was draining Papa and he was planning on getting out. He first sold the restaurant portion of the shop in the hope of making the bakery a success by having to look after only the one side of the business.

We had some customers from Keesler Air Force Base from among whom Grandma made one of her best friends. She was a female sergeant in the US Air Force, Sergeant Tosh. Sergeant Tosh proved to be a great friend to Grandma and kept in touch with her after she left Keesler for a Japan posting. She sent Grandma many treasures from the Far East. Grandma received very ornate china dinner and tea sets from her. I remember that Grandma had some Japanese tea cups that were so thin that the light would come through them. Some cups even had pictures hidden in the base that were apparent only when the cup was held up to a light. This was very different from the toys that were then made in Japan. Defeated in the war, Japan was trying hard to recover and had become a manufactory for cheap goods for the world. Japanese manufactured goods were of very poor quality. Any Japanese-made toy would soon break. It took Japan a long time to overcome this stigma. It was a paradox: how could the country produce such fine craftsmanship in its china when it manufactured other poor quality products such as toys.

My experience at the elementary school that was next door to the bakery was not good. Memories of the actual class are few, but I do remember that the school had an Easter egg hunt before Easter. I didn't find many eggs during the formal school hunt, but after school I went back into the school grounds and did my own search. To my great surprise, I found several eggs that had been missed during the day. To me, this was treasure.

During the rest of that year, I caught chicken-pox and many of the colds and flu viruses going round. As a result of changing school three times in first grade and having to stay home with infections, I had the honor of failing the first grade. I once had a friend ask me how I failed crayons and sleep time.

CHAPTER THREE

BACK TO GULFPORT

PAPA finally got back his job at the Veterans Affairs hospital as a nurse's aide and gave up the bakery in Biloxi. He moved all the ovens and his bakery equipment into a shed behind our house in Gulfport. I guess that he thought that one day he would again try to open a bakery.

Papa's life reverted to the routine of the evening shift at the VA hospital and tending his garden. Papa was my hero, my role model and my mentor, and I loved him as much as any son could ever possibly love a father. Sometimes he would take me to the Longinos' corner store on the corner of 23rd Street and Hewes Avenue and treat me to a Coke, which cost the princely sum of five cents. I remember walking down 23rd Street to the Hewes Avenue store behind Papa, trying to keep in the footsteps he made on the dirt road.

Life once again felt normal for me and I started back in the first grade of the Northeast Elementary School where I had been in September the year before. It just seemed as if time had stood still for a year. The only difference was that I was now with a different set of students who were one year younger than me.

I soon also became aware of a handicap that I had. Up until then, being left-handed had not made much difference, but I was invited to join a Pee Wee league baseball team by Phil Bolton, our teenage neighbor from the end of Searle Avenue who was coaching the team. Not being able to afford a glove, I was loaned one by Phil. It was a catcher's mitt and I was first put in as catcher. In my first game I caught the ball and I had to take off the mitt to throw the ball with my left hand. In this first game, one of the batters hit a foul and I was surprised when I put up the mitt and the ball landed directly in it sending the batter out. The euphoria soon wore off since it was apparent that I could not function as a catcher with a right-hand catcher's mitt. I was tried in many positions on the team such as second base and short stop but ended up in right field. I would borrow gloves but tried to wear them on my right hand. I remember going to a friend's house to watch the World Series on his family's television. Everyone there was wearing a baseball glove except me. I tried

14

very hard to fit in with the baseball crowd but I was a misfit. One day while playing baseball, one of the neighborhood boys got on his hands and knees behind me and another boy pushed me on the chest, so that I fell over the boy behind. It was apparent that I was not wanted, so I went home and never joined them again.

Of the people still alive at this time whom Grandma had raised, all were left-handed except Uncle Buster. Mom told me that Grandma had told her that she was cursed because she picked on her brother, Uncle Guy, so much as a kid for being left-handed. I wonder if our left-handedness was a self-fulfilling prophecy of Grandma's and that she had perhaps unconsciously trained us this way, since I would shoot a rifle right-handed and drew a bow right-handed. All my brothers and sisters are right-handed and there are a lot of us!

Soon after I left Jackson, Mom gave birth to my brother Joey, but tragedy struck during the Christmas season in 1951 when Joey died of meningitis; he had contracted an ear infection that spread to the lining of his brain. I never saw my brother Joey alive. I was told that the Christmas tree was decorated, the lights were up and that Joey was smiling and pointing to the illuminations, eating ice cream and generally enjoying the family's festivities. Then sometime around 3:00 am, he started to cry uncontrollably and the family realized that there was something major wrong with him. Mom and Dad rushed Joey to the hospital but he was dead by daylight. Even though I was not there this had a profound effect on me, and when a father, with my own children, I was always afraid when one of my boys got an ear infection.

Joey's body was brought back to Gulfport for his funeral. As a seven-year-old, I could not understand the meaning of death or the impact on Mom. At Joey's burial, Mom broke down totally and started to cry hysterically. At the graveside, she tried to open the coffin crying, "I want my baby back." I broke into tears, not for Joey – I never knew Joey – but for the pain I saw in Mom. Mom's pain was suddenly mine. Mom once told me that she was cursed by having too much love. She surely had a soft heart. However, I believe that Joey's grave has seldom if ever been visited since his burial till this day. I learned later that my Uncle Buster did have a good side to him since he had taken care of the funeral arrangements and even purchased Joey's grave. I was glad to learn this, since in my youth I always looked upon him as pure evil.

It was the summer of 1951, and Mom and Dad came back to Gulfport and stayed with Uncle Sam and Aunt Sid for a while. They had started to build a house on the one-acre lot that Papa had sold them from his three-acre parcel. The lot was only cleared for a house pad with a small space around it. The rest of the plot remained wooded. The house was small and was cramped with both Uncle Sam and Aunt Sid's and Mom and Dad's family in it. Altogether there were four adults and five kids living there. Uncle Sam's house was small and cute, but it was unfinished. I continued to live with Grandma and Papa in the house next door.

Dad got himself a job working for Bond Bread Bakery as a delivery man. I rode with him several mornings on his route out from Gulfport to behind Biloxi, and marveled at the beauty of the Gulf Coast area. The bayous and the live oak trees with their hanging Spanish moss were spectacular in the early mornings at sunrise. Every day after his deliveries, Dad would bring the delivery truck home to Uncle Sam's house and keep it there till the next morning when he would go to the bakery to collect the goods he needed to deliver that day.

During this time in Gulfport, I once found a folded five dollar bill on the ground in front of Aunt Sid's house. In my excitement, I rushed in to show my aunt my newly found treasure. I was told that Aunt Sid had lost the bill a while back and that I should return it. It was with much reluctance that I handed over the money. As a reward, Aunt Sid gave me twenty-five cents and let me draw down on it five cents at a time. It seemed unfair to me in some ways; I had experienced the euphoria of newly found treasure and then it was suddenly taken away. However, it turned out okay since I could go twice to the Longinos' store and buy one of my favorite candy bars, a Butterfinger bar, and a Coke as each was only five cents. I had a nickel left over and must have bought either another Butterfinger or a Coke with it.

My brothers and sisters and our cousins and I would play in front of Uncle Sam's house and we were little devils. On one occasion, we filled the gas tank of Dad's car, which was parked out front of Uncle Sam's house, with sand. This did not please Dad too much. However, since I was living with Grandma and

Papa I was able to find my way home before experiencing his rage. I was the oldest in the group and I would have taken the brunt of any blame.

Since I was not with the family much, my sister Sue became the family's Alpha Child. I enjoyed it when she would give me her attention and I would follow her instructions. On one occasion, my sister Sue and I were playing with a newspaper and matches in the woods behind Uncle Sam's house trying to start a fire. We laid the newspaper flat on the ground and lit it. However, this proved not to be a good method to get a fire going since the paper would just burn a little and then go out. Finally, by adding leaves on top of newspaper, we were successful. We were so successful that we set fire to the wood; this turned out to be somewhat devastating since it developed into a major fire and burned the woods badly. It must have been on a rare occasion, when it was dry, since I recall it being very rainy and wet most of the time, conditions that would not sustain a fire in the green woods. I went home and hid behind Grandma's red vinyl couch to avoid the Fire Department. I was very frightened when I heard what I thought was a fireman come to the front door. It turned out to be only a paranoid reaction since the visitor was not related to the fire. All in all, we were little kids with too much time and energy on our hands.

Dad had aspirations to be a famous Country and Western musician and I remember hearing Country and Western music coming from Uncle Sam's house as Dad and his friends would jam. This could have been from envy of Uncle Sam who was a successful band leader. Dad loved honky-tonks and juke joints. He had a drinking problem and was constantly seeking wine (or in his case, beer), women and song. I'm not sure if he had any success in getting a paying gig as a musician, but I know that he would find jam sessions wherever he could.

During my time in Gulfport I tried several experiments, proving that I still did not have a great understanding of the principles of physics. The first was jumping off the roof of Papa and Grandma's house with an umbrella. For a seven-year-old boy it is a long ways down and I hit the ground with a lot more force than I had wished for. The umbrella proved to be useless in slowing my fall.

I had befriended a neighborhood boy who liked to swim in the pool of the Markham Hotel,[1] a once-grand hotel in downtown Gulfport. He was a good swimmer and I started going regularly to the pool with him as Mom was a check-out clerk for a supermarket across the street from the hotel. The pool was on the roof of the building. I was teaching myself to swim by keeping close to the edge of the pool so I could grab onto the handrail whenever I panicked. One of our experiments involved cutting a section of garden hose about two-feet long so that I could stand on the bottom of the pool and breathe through the hose. Again, initial theory proved to be wrong. When my friend and I next went to the Markham Hotel pool, I jumped into the deep end to try the experiment and found to my surprise that I could not breathe through the hose. I had not yet learned that water pressure in deep water is much greater than at the surface and I was unable to draw breath through the hosing. In panic, I rose up and grabbed onto the pool side. Abandoning the hose I went back to my crude method of trying to teach myself to swim. Eventually, I could swim the length of the pool without grabbing onto the rail.

One day after a swim with my friend I went to meet Mom at the supermarket where she was working. I was feeling very unwell. I sat in a corner on the floor feeling awful waiting for Mom to get off and take me home to Papa and Grandma's house. When Mom took me home it was realized that I had developed measles, a common childhood disease that I had missed at school the previous year. I had a very high fever and was immediately put to bed. Grandma called a doctor who came to the house to see if he could do anything. The fever was causing me to slip in and out of a dream world and I lost the reality of where I was in my bed at Grandma's house. There was little to be done except to give me aspirin to break the fever. I had a rash all over my body, and a bad cough and running nose. Grandma kept canaries and I remember hearing one of them singing as the fever broke for the final time. It felt as if I had returned from the dead. The subsequent discussion among the adults was that I had caught a

---

[1] The Markham Hotel remains in Gulfport, but since damage caused by Hurricane Katrina it faces an uncertain future.

particularly bad dose of measles because of my outings to the swimming pool.

Later, Mom and Dad got their own house and Mom became pregnant again; this time it was with my sister Kitty. Mom was ashamed to tell Grandma, since she was having a baby nearly every year. Dad did his rolling stone thing again and went off to California. After less than a year, Mom did her normal thing and found out where he was and followed. I was left with Grandma and Papa. By now I was calling myself Junior Douglas, since Douglas was my grandparents' family name and Junior was my nickname. I saw Grandma and Papa as my parents and I asked them if I could change my name to theirs. They contemplated this but never did anything about it.

I had visions of becoming a preacher and Sister Lee allowed me to deliver a sermon to her congregation. I had picked John, chapter 3, verse 16 as the basis of my sermon: "For God so loved the world that he gave his only begotten son...." It was a great shock to me to realize that after much preparation I was in the pulpit for only a little over eight or nine minutes instead of the twenty that was allotted for my sermon. I was to remember this when I started to lecture in university many years later.

Directly across Searle Avenue from us lived the Empt family. They were a family of three: Mr. and Mrs. Empt and a teenage daughter named Marcia. The Empts were great neighbors. I believe that Mr. Empt had retired from New York. They also had a large three-acre plot with a pecan orchard that doubled as a sheep pasture. Mr. Empt had quite a number of pecan trees in his orchard. Grandma had worked out a deal with the Empts to use their washing machine, which was kept in a barn behind their house. Once a week grandma would take our dirty laundry to the Empt's barn and use their electric tub. Everything on the machine was manual. It was an old-fashioned machine with a wash tub equipped with an agitator and a separate wringer consisting of two rollers that would squeeze the water from the laundry. However, it was better than doing it by hand and Grandma would wash all our laundry in the Empt's machine.

Mrs. Empt was an artist and Grandma had a couple of her paintings hanging in our house. I was particularly taken with a watercolor of a bunch of bananas still on the tree. Grandma also had a beautiful painting of a magnolia blossom which Mrs. Empt had done.

Mr. Empt would allow me to hunt squirrels in the pecan trees in his orchard with my Daisy Red Ryder BB Gun. Being a New Yorker, Mr. Empt saw squirrels only as vermin, but to us a squirrel was meat on the table. Mr. Empt disliked the squirrels because they ate his pecans. Everyone considered it was very ambitious of me to think that I could kill a squirrel with a BB gun. However, one day I actually did, which earned me much praise and admiration from Mr. Empt. I remember him bragging to the milkman doing his morning delivery of milk on our street about my marksmanship. The hunt was exciting, but I remember taking the squirrel home and sitting on the front porch looking at its dead body and the hollow feeling it caused inside me. I felt the finality of death that I had inflicted and the sense of emptiness it leaves you when you kill. It brought me to tears.

As a result of my marksmanship, in June 1953 Grandma and Papa bought me a Remington .22 single shot rifle for my ninth birthday. One day, I was in the living room reading a children's book and heard Grandma shooting at a couple of squirrels that were in the big oak tree in our front yard with my rifle. I went out to investigate and since the rifle was mine she gave it to me after missing several times. I loaded the single shot rifle and aimed at one of the squirrels (from my right shoulder) that was making a run for it across a branch about twenty feet up. I shot and saw a trail of smoke reach the squirrel but the animal kept running. As I anxiously started to load the rifle again, the squirrel ran about five feet along the branch and then fell out of the tree. When we went over to the squirrel we found it was dead; the bullet had gone straight through it and crushed its heart. The shot did not provide enough impact to knock the squirrel out of the tree and it must have been alive for the five feet it ran along the branch before falling to its death. This squirrel was not around long enough for me to feel sorry for it; Grandma dressed it out very quickly and chicken-fried it for supper.

By now Uncle Sam had sold his house to a couple whom I recall as being young and very religious and going by the name of Davis. At nine years old, I remember the woman to have been very striking looking, slim and with red hair. The Davis family called the police about us using a rifle in the city limits. A few hours later the police showed up and counseled us on the dangers of shooting in a populated area. In reality, we were in a wooded area and my grandparents being farmers did not understand the fuss. The police threatened to take away my rifle if it happened again. I sat in the living room in the single vinyl covered red chair holding my rifle and crying over the possibility of not being able to use my new birthday present, or if I did, of losing it forever. This sort of ended my overt hunting days in Gulfport, at least the shooting of squirrels in front of the house.

CHAPTER FOUR

CALIFORNIA

IT was the summer of 1953 and Mr. Empt allowed me to hunt in his pecan orchard with my new .22 rifle, which I would do early in the morning to avoid detection. Grandma and Mom were talking together about me going to California to live with Mom and Dad again. Mom claimed that she really missed me and pressured Grandma. The decision as to whether I should stay with my grandparents or go to California was given to me, a nine-year-old boy. As a nine-year-old, I looked upon the possibility as an adventure and said I wished to move back to live with Mom and Dad.

Grandma and I caught the train from Gulfport to New Orleans to connect with the Sunset Limited to Los Angeles. The train ride from New Orleans to LA took three days. The seats were in a car arranged similarly to a bus, except in some places seats would face each other with more space. Grandma had packed enough food for the two of us to eat for the journey in a cardboard box that she had got from the Longinos' store, since train food was too expensive.

Across from us was a black man, which I found unusual since in Gulfport all the buses were segregated. Grandma and the man struck up a conversation and she explained that I was her grandson and she was taking me to stay with my family in California. He was from New Orleans and was going to California to be with a son who had earlier taken his family to LA. I'll never forget his words: "California, that's God's country! It's the land of milk and honey." The man was going to the Promised Land to start a new life with a son who had left New Orleans some years before. This reinforced my view that the decision I had made to accept my Mom's offer to return to the family and live in California was a good one.

After less than a day's travel we were in Texas. As we crossed Texas, I was amazed by what I saw. The landscape changed totally from its familiar green to the light-brown of the desert. I felt that something was missing. I longed to see the green landscape of Mississippi. The train continued on through New Mexico and into Arizona. In Tucson, Arizona, the landscape looked familiar, because of the cowboy TV shows that I had sneaked out to neighbors' houses in Gulfport to see. The light-brown dry desert and tall cactuses could have been a set for many of the Hopalong Cassidy, Roy Rogers or Lone Ranger TV shows.

We finally arrived at the train station in LA, where we were met by Mom and Dad. Compared with Gulfport, LA was huge and had many many more cars. We went to Mom and Dad's house on East 5th Street close to Rowan Avenue in East LA. Mom and Dad had rented a house in what was the largest Mexican barrio of the US. East 5th Street was down a steep hill off Rowan Avenue and we had to use steps to walk uphill to get to the house. The house was bigger than Papa and Grandma's and I thought, as a new home, it looked nice. It the front area down the hill toward East 5th Street there was a large avocado tree that had fruit on it. I had never seen an avocado so it was fascinating to me.

Grandma stayed for a couple of days and took the same train journey in reverse back to Gulfport. In later life she told me that she nearly died from heartache when she left. I remember that when she left for the station I was sitting at the dining table with tears in my eyes. Mom gave me a Coke to try and calm me down. I was now for the first time questioning my decision to move back in with the family.

I again found myself moving from being the only child to the oldest of a large family. There were five of us now, with the addition of Kitty. The environment was totally different from what I was used to. We had television here, and whereas in Gulfport I had an occasional Coke bought by Papa, here we had Hostess Twinkies and Ding Dongs, and a big variety of cereals such as Kellogg's Sugar Frosted Flakes, and Coco Puffs. Perhaps the black man on the train was right; I had moved to the land of milk and honey. I went from a much disciplined life that was regimented by Grandma to total freedom. As kids, we were like a pack of wild dogs with very few restrictions. If I wanted, I could watch television all night. If we had a disagreement, we had to settle it ourselves. Sue still had the role of Alpha Child in the family; Dad and Mom both worked and left us to our own devices. We made The Simpsons look like a loving functional family.

I was fascinated by the hills of California. In Mississippi the land was flat. East 5th Street from Rowan Avenue was a very steep hill. There were a couple of old bicycles in the house and once I attempted to ride the hill down East 5th Street. I used the front brakes when the bike began to go too fast for me to handle and I was – inevitably – thrown over the handlebars and crashed into a telephone pole. I was sore for days.

I started at school at Rowan Avenue Elementary School and was told that I was too old for the fourth grade and was put directly into the fifth grade. The LA schools of the time had a system of stepping the kids through by age.

Socially, school started out okay for me. I found the kids in East LA to be easy to get along with even though they would speak Spanish to each other. Class was difficult since I had missed instruction in short division in the fourth grade and the class was going directly into long division. Also, there was no family pressure to study and I would go home and turn on the television set and spend all my waking hours watching TV.

One day toward the end of the school year, the teacher and some kids were standing staring out of the window of our classroom. I joined the crowd at the window and saw a large cloud of smoke coming from the direction of where our rented house was. A couple of the students who knew where I lived said they thought that it was my house. I disagreed, but when I went home I found that it was indeed my house. It was quite a shock to see the damage. The walls were still standing but everything inside was ruined. If something was not burned, it was destroyed by the smell of smoke or the water used to put out the fire. The Fire Department could not locate the source of the fire and thought it might have been caused by an electrical short, but Mom told me that she believed that Doug and Sandy had been playing with fire and had started the blaze. My sister Sue and I were in school but luckily Mom was home to get all the kids out. Sandy was home from school sick and she told me later that while she was in bed in her room she had seen Doug run by very quickly and went to investigate and found the kitchen on fire. She ran out of the house as well. Being at home at the time, Mom was able to see that Kitty got out.

Our neighbors really came to our aid after this. We were given blankets, food and clothing, and were taken in to have a place to sleep. The other kids and I, except Kitty, were taken in by a newly-wed couple who were about to go visit their relatives in celebration of their wedding. Another family took in Mom, Dad and Kitty. The community spirit of East LA was amazing. Dad would always call them "wetbacks" but they were very decent folks who demonstrated a great spirit of charity and humanity. Perhaps this is why, to this day, East LA still feels like home.

CHAPTER FIVE

BACK TO GRANDMA'S HOUSE

THE newly wedded couple that had taken in us kids after the fire, whose names I believe were Daniel and Maria, were about to take a trip to Juarez, Mexico, just south of El Paso in Texas. They were going to visit Maria's family to introduce her new husband to them. Mom had asked them if they could deliver us to Gulfport en route and they agreed to take us kids, minus Kitty, to stay with Papa and Grandma. I think that Mom had paid them some expenses for the trip, but I'm not sure of the exact arrangements that were made. The plan was that while Mom and Dad tried to find a new place to live and settle in, we would be in Gulfport with Grandma and Papa waiting for them to come and get us when everything was in order.

It was to prove a long car journey and we left very early in the morning before sunrise. It was May and the only timely thing about the fire was that school was about to be out for the summer, freeing us from the need to go to school. The journey took us through Southern California, Arizona and New Mexico. We arrived in Juarez in the late evening after what seemed to be an eternity of boring desert scenery.

The stopover in Juarez, Mexico, was for one and a half days, mainly allowing for rest but also for Maria initially to introduce her new husband to her family before continuing the final leg of our journey to Gulfport. To me it was a great experience, visiting with the family in Mexico, even if I could not speak Spanish. Maria's family was warm and reminded me of Grandma and Papa but in a different way. The language and food were different, but the family feeling was the same. The family residence was one of many houses surrounding a courtyard with a well in the center. The atmosphere was totally different from that on the US side of the border. It amazed me how just a few hundred yards either side of an international crossing could make such a difference. If we went out of the courtyard we could see El Paso across the Rio Grande: two very different worlds divided only by culture and an agreed border.

It seemed that everything centered on the well: from drinking water and washing dishes to laundry and bathing. It was the source of water for the micro community and a special place. I was fascinated by Mexican culture. It was poor for sure, but still there was a strong sense of family and community that even I could feel as a young boy about to be ten years old.

The final leg of our journey again started before sunrise. I was expecting it to take the same time as the first half, but this leg proved to be a lot longer. The journey took us through San Antonio then to Houston. As kids, by the time we reached San Antonio we were already very bored with the scenery and being cooped up in a car. However, we remained on our best behavior since we did not know the couple well enough to make a scene. As we got closer to Houston, the environment began to change; it started to become flatter and greener. Also, I started to feel the familiar summer humidity. It was nice, like going back into the familiar womb of my birthplace. As we approached the Louisiana border, I began falling asleep. It was a surreal experience of moving back into a familiar environment of green trees and grass; I was going home again.

Louisiana was a blur to me and I only remember going over the very tall bridge that crossed the Mississippi River in New Orleans. I woke up for a moment and saw the height of the bridge and the darkness below with the lights of ships going in and out of New Orleans.

We finally arrived at the house on Searle Avenue in Gulfport and Papa and Grandma were already asleep. Maria knocked on the front door and woke Papa and Grandma up while we waited in the car. It must have been well after midnight since Papa was home from work. They were expecting us and invited us in quickly. Papa and Grandma had made sleeping arrangements for everyone. I was to go back to my familiar bed in Papa and Grandma's room and the other three kids had beds set up in the extension built by Papa at the back of our "shotgun" house. Sandy and Sue had to sleep together and Doug had his own bed. Maria and Daniel had the familiar red vinyl couch in the living room that folded down into a bed. Since it was really late, we all retired to our assigned sleeping places soon after arrival. Back in my bed again it was as if I had never left and the year in California was only a dream. I was soon asleep in the familiar surroundings.

The next morning I awoke to a familiar environment but with the excitement and fatigue of having just taken the long car trip from Los Angeles to Gulfport. I was groggy since my biological clock had not adjusted to Gulfport time. Maria and Daniel were going to stay a day to rest up and see some of the sights of the place. After one of Grandma's big breakfasts of eggs, bacon, grits and her famous biscuits, I first sat around still dazed from the long journey while the adults chatted and my brother and sisters roamed around exploring Papa and Grandma's house.

After our breakfasts had settled we went off for a car tour of Gulfport. Maria and Daniel took us kids only with them since there was no room in their car for Papa and Grandma. We drove down Searle Avenue, across the railroad tracks and the middle class section of 2nd Avenue, and then to Highway 90. We turned toward downtown Gulfport and traveled along Highway 90 toward the center looking at all the big waterfront mansions that were on one side of the highway and the world's largest manmade beach on the other. Both sides were great scenery in the clear morning sun. As a kid I always dreamed of living in one of the fine houses on Highway 90. Most of these big fine homes had large live oak trees and Spanish moss blowing gently in the gulf breeze. Most also had big front porches and tall columns that looked as if they might belong on the White House in Washington DC.

Gulfport in 1953 was not a big place and we drove to the main pier in its center to see some of the yachts that were tied up there. The tour took us only to dinner (as Papa and Grandma called the noon meal; the evening meal was known as supper). After sitting down to large portions of Grandma's Southern fried chicken, black-eyed peas, cornbread, fresh tomatoes and sliced onions, Papa, Grandma and I retired, as was a custom, for a noon nap. Maria, Daniel and my brother and sisters were not used to sleeping at noon so they stayed up.

Papa and Grandma and I got up after an hour and Papa prepared to report to his job as a nurse's aid. Papa had to be there at 2:00 pm so set off as usual at 1:15 pm, walking down Searle Avenue toward the Veterans Affairs hospital.

Maria and Daniel just sat around the house and rested as they wished to leave the next morning to do the leg that we had just completed together, but in reverse. Evening meals at Papa and

Grandma's house were always very light and as oftentimes this one consisted of a piece of cornbread and a glass of milk. We retired for bed at around 7:30 since there was no television to watch. This was okay with Maria and Daniel since they were planning to get an early start before sunrise on the journey back to Juarez to continue their family visit. Also, our biological clocks were still on California time, making it seem like three hours later anyway.

The following morning, when I woke up, I remember being sad at not having seen Maria and Daniel leave. I had grown fond of them at their house on East 5th Street and the journey had had a bonding effect on me. Looking back it makes me sad that I never saw them again. It was odd the way that we were brought together by the fire and just as suddenly we broke apart, but we had been as close as a family for a few days.

Life that summer at Papa and Grandma's soon fell into a routine. I felt at home again, but my brother Doug and my sisters Sue and Sandy learned to dislike me since I was Grandma's pet and she gave me special attention. Also, Sue, who was the Alpha Child of the family back in California, hated me more than the other two when she found she was now in a place where I was the king of the hill.

One incident that remains very vivid took place at supper one evening while we were eating oatmeal. Sue said something I did not like so I filled my spoon with oatmeal and held it in a threatening position so that I could catapult the contents of the spoon toward her with both hands. She dared me to go ahead and fling the oatmeal at her, calling me chicken. Hearing the dare, I launched the oatmeal for a perfect hit in her face. For the first time, I saw her break down in tears rather than try and destroy me physically. This was too much for Grandma, who would normally side with me. Grandma did not say anything but went and got one of Papa's leather belts and gave me two well-placed blows across my back. This had me in tears with the pain of the whacks.

We spent that summer largely by playing in the yard of Papa and Grandma's house waiting for Mom and Dad to come and collect us. The property was now only one acre in size since Papa had sold a second acre, this time to cousins Suzy and Renee.

Cousins Suzy and Renee were two old maids and I do not remember if they were from Papa's or Grandma's side of the family. Anyway, with the acre gone, Papa's land was now reduced to a cultivated area with a chicken coop and the storage facility containing Papa's bakery equipment; regardless, it made an excellent playground for us. Papa did not need the original three acres and was able to provide for the family well with his one-acre garden.

One day while I was at Grandma's, Grandma was called on the telephone and I was told to go up to cousins Suzy and Renee's house as a large wild rabbit had been seen in the woods out front there. I took my .22 rifle and went to their front porch and could see the rabbit foraging in the undergrowth. I loaded a .22 Long Rifle cartridge and started to stalk the rabbit. I got close enough and had a clear shot and fired. I hit the rabbit in the stomach and it did a 360-degree flip from the impact of the bullet and started to run. I began to chase it to finish it off but it was able to get away. It gave me a bad feeling to wound an animal and not be able to finish it. I'm sure that it must have died a slow painful death from the wound.

It was in early August that Mom and Dad came for us. We did the trip back to California by car again. The only memories that still come to mind are that in the middle of the trip we stayed in a motel to rest up and it had a swimming pool. Also, I recall going through Arizona and visiting the Petrified Forest, the Painted Desert and the Meteor Crater, and that on the trip outside of Flagstaff there was a road that was so steep that you could see cars above and below you. It was beautiful, especially as we were on the road around sunset. It was a great trip back and it gave the feeling of a vacation rather than a return from a disaster.

CHAPTER SIX

MONTEBELLO

WE arrived at our new accommodation, which was now in Montebello. Dad and Mom had rented a two-bedroom apartment across from Freemont Elementary school. The apartment complex was on 2nd Street and I can still picture its lawn and the school grounds across the street. The several buildings that made up the apartment complex were two stories high and had four units in each. We had a ground-floor apartment and Mom and Dad had one of the bedrooms while the three girls had the other. My brother Doug and I had the living room. It was much smaller than the house in East Los Angeles.

I started the sixth grade at Freemont Elementary School and found the new school to be a lot more similar to the one that I had left in Gulfport than the one I'd been at in East LA – in that I was not in a minority. The only difference was that the school in Gulfport did not have any Mexican kids at all whereas the few Mexicans in Montebello were a minority at the school. It was a white-dominated school for sure. In East LA, the vast majority of the kids were Mexican and as a nine-year-old I had had no trouble getting along. However, this new school turned out to be a major culture shock. The kids looked like me but they were in fact very different. I still had a heavy Southern drawl and that instantly set me apart from the rest of the class. My grandparents' influence had made me profoundly religious and although I desperately wanted to fit in, many times this singled me out to be picked on. I cannot remember making any really close friends during this episode in my life.

I recall that once when in the playground after school, one of the school bullies wrestled me to the ground and tried to force me to use swear words. Being a good Christian, I refused and took the physical abuse. On another occasion, my strict Christianity caused me to lose a possible friend when he told his mom about a conversation that we'd had when I expressed my Christian views. He later told me that he could not play with me anymore and his mom had called me "that weirdo." It seemed as if my religious beliefs were at odds with everyone. I would still make attempts to fit in, but continued to feel my beliefs should not be sacrificed.

After several months of being at the new school, I was in an after-school pickup baseball game where the bully that had tested my beliefs earlier was on the same team. I had developed a little coordination since my unpleasant Gulfport experience with baseball. I was at bat and hit a great fly ball that was missed by the left outfielder; I looked at the bully and said, "Look at that God damn ball go." He looked back with a smile of victory. I had been broken; I backslid and I felt that I was going to fit in finally. However, this was at a heavy price, I had betrayed my God and major beliefs to fit in. The peer pressure of the kids was a far more powerful influence than my religion.

As time passed my heavy Southern drawl was slowly replaced by the standard California accent of Montebello and I was finding my way into the pecking order. I had joined the Boy Scouts and tried to collect merit badges, but my family did not have the money to support my scouting activities in a way that was needed. I guess I should feel grateful that they did buy a uniform for me. I remember going camping at a Scout Jubilee in the Southern California area with my troop and having a cast iron frying pan and a plate from Mom's kitchen as an improvised mess kit, while all the other kids had nice Scout mess kits. With five kids in the family I did not get the same support that I was accustomed to having with my grandparents. I progressed a little in the Boy Scouts, winning an occasional merit badge.

The big scouting experience for me was the opening of Disneyland in July 1955. There was a large celebration held at the LA Coliseum marking the opening of Disneyland, with many of the Scouts from my troop getting to play Indians in one scene of the day's show. I remember dressing up as an Indian brave and participating in the war scene at the Coliseum, where hundreds of us – from my own and many other troops – were dressed as Native American warriors to do our simulated attack on the settlers, also played by Scouts. It was a great feeling to take part in the performance. Some of us were supposed to pretend to be shot by the settlers and fall to the ground and act as if we were dead. I was proud to be chosen as one to be killed and put on a great performance of being shot and falling to the ground. Of course, the settlers won in the end. At the end of the simulated war we all got up to a great round of applause from the audience as we cleared out the Coliseum for the next event of the celebration. The event was filmed and parts were played on the Mickey Mouse TV show.

During this phase of my life, I was never much of a superstar either academically or athletically. The only thing that was notable is that in the sixth grade we were given a hearing test and I had a perfect score along with only one other kid in the class. I was asked to join the school glee club since I should be able to hear the differences in music. I remember the glee club performing toward the end of the sixth-grade school year and that I wore black pants and a freshly ironed white shirt that Mom had bought for the performance. I was a soprano and although I had no solo part Mom had made a point of going to the performance. I remember how proud I felt seeing my mom in the audience. I graduated from Freemont Elementary in June 1955.

In September 1955, I started at Montebello Junior High School, now Montebello Intermediate School. It was an amazing time since I was starting my second year straight in the same school system. However, I still did not totally fit in. The school used to have lunch packs for sale and my favorite was the hotdog pack, which cost twenty-five cents. It consisted of a hotdog, a large cookie, an orange and a carton of milk. I was sitting on the lawn one day savoring a school-bought hotdog lunch pack when two very cute girls sat down close to me and I heard one looking at me saying, "He's cute," and giggling. It made me very uncomfortable so instead of making the most of it I got up and moved away. I was very shy when it came to girls. At the time I wished that I had the courage to go over and talk to them.

My dad's love of administering corporal punishment to me was still there. I was belted one time for I cannot remember what and while in a physical education class a fellow student questioned the belt bursa that was showing at the edge of my PE shorts. In defense I replied, "I deserved it." I guess that I had to accept it to continue to live with the family.

Seventh grade was uneventful and I blended into the crowd as much as I could. Not to be seen was a way of avoiding confrontation with fellow students. The most memorable thing about the seventh grade was that I learned to love the hamburgers and Cherry Cokes at a soda fountain across Whittier

Boulevard from the school. When I could get enough money together by not buying a lunch pack, I would buy a hamburger and a Cherry Coke in preference to what I had already been given.

In the summer of 1957, Mom and Dad moved to a different part of Montebello and I had to change schools yet again. I was now attending the eighth grade at Eastmont Junior High, now Eastmont Intermediate School. By this time I'd perfected the art of being a chameleon and not being noticed at school, so I was able to get through the school year without much trauma.

During this year I tried to run away and go home to Gulfport. I'm not sure what reasoning led to my action, but I packed the army surplus pack that I used in the Boy Scouts with a few cans of beans, filled a canteen with water and started walking down the railroad track toward the east. I figured the train tracks should lead to New Orleans and from there I could find the tracks that led to Gulfport. I was hoping that I would be able to get on a freight train when it slowed down. After about five hours of walking down the tracks and having trains roar past me as if I was not there, I came to the conclusion that this was not a well-thought-out plan and decided to get back home to my parents' apartment. While walking back I came to a railroad crossing and saw a sheriff's police car; I waved it down and turned myself in. I was taken to the local station and my parents were called. I had made a good distance considering I was only on foot, but I was still in LA County. Mom and Dad came and picked me up. I was expecting to get belted for the adventure but was spared. It seemed as if they were aware that I was unhappy in California and I was shown mercy.

CHAPTER SEVEN

BACK TO EAST LOS ANGELES

IN summer 1958, we moved again. This time, we went from an apartment to a nice three-bedroom house in East Los Angeles, very close to Monterey Park, which was at the far edge of the Mexican barrio. It was a beautiful house with a large empty field in front and across the field you could see Atlantic Boulevard. For the first time Doug and I shared a proper bedroom and the three girls had a bedroom for themselves. It was nice to have the additional space of an extra bedroom.

Mom had begun to work for a supermarket that was within walking distance of the house. In September I had to start the ninth grade at Griffith Junior High, now Griffith Middle School. The return to a school with a majority of Mexican students was not a bad feeling since I had started my life in California a few years earlier in such a school. My three years in Montebello had not been exactly a great school experience and this was a new start for me.

At Griffith I was determined that I was going to fit in. After a few weeks there, I was beginning to make some friends. One in particular was Manuel whom I met in the physical education class. He was a little taller than me and had started to grow a beard. At this time I had just an occasional whisker and was jealous of his beard. It was only in my early twenties that I sported such a beard. He used jokily to make fun of the fact that I still had not reached full puberty. His jokes were made in a good spirited way, not what I had been used to in Montebello. Our friendship did not involve going to each other's houses, but it was nice to have someone to be at ease around.

My class prior to lunch was metal shop and we were learning metal working. There was a bully in this class who kept picking on me when the teacher was not looking. It was a situation similar to that which I had endured in my Montebello days. One day he came up behind me with a paint brush and brushed a strip of black paint across the back of my trousers. I verbally confronted him for this and he pushed me. I pushed back and a fight started. This was the first time that I had physically defended myself and found that I was able to block his blows and got in a few good ones on him before the teacher realized what had happened and broke up the fight. The whole class was amused by the altercation. Since no one was seriously hurt the teacher just had a talk with us and did not take further action except to tell the boys' vice-principal, who talked to me, and (I assumed) talked to the bully. During lunch that same day and several days after, some of the other boys in the class would approach me saying, "Come on, *esé*, we need to finish this in the toilets." (*Esé* in Latino parlance meant something like chum or dude.)

On the day of the fight, Manuel learned of the altercation since the news had spread like wildfire and he quickly found me. He advised me not to listen to the boys and to stay out of the toilets. He said that the bully's friends were planning on "jumping" me in the toilets or after school when I was walking home. For several days after school he met and walked with me till I got a safe distance from the school on my way home. He was a true friend and yet was not that close; it was a great feeling to have someone who cared for me as a fellow creature.

The aftermath of the altercation cleared quickly; I was not bothered again by the bully and I quickly started to try and fit in. An important thing in achieving this was the clothing you wore. The dress for boys at Griffith in those days was a purple Sir Guy shirt, Chino pants, shoes highly polished by spit-shining and a white tee-shirt. The Sir Guy shirt was not to be worn but draped over the arm and carried. Of course in school the shirt had to be worn, but after school on the streets the shirt was draped over the arm. I started to save money to accumulate the proper clothes for this new culture. I understand why the Sir Guy was draped since it was an expensive item and a status symbol, pretty much as mobile phones are today. It was not to be worn and gotten sweaty. By mid-year I had accumulated the proper attire and was very proud to walk down the street with my Sir Guy shirt draped on my arm. My year at Griffith had been good with the exception of the altercation and I graduated from Junior High in summer 1959 with a great feeling of accomplishment.

Fall 1959 was the start of high school at Garfield High. For a teen, high school is one of the last obstacles prior to becoming an adult. It never seemed to me like the movies, with cars and romance; rather, for me, it was a hard time – you are not yet an adult but still there are higher expectations. However, you had to progress through the grades and each grade gave you a little more status. I was with the class that was scheduled to graduate in the summer of 1962. We chose a class name, the "Orithyians," and our class colors were beige and brown. We could buy a class sweater, which I admired very much, but because of family finances I never did get a sweater of my own.

Perhaps because of the semi-positive influence of the Boy Scouts earlier, I joined the Junior Reserve Officers' Training Corps (JROTC), which we were allowed to do in place of physical education. Also, I remember seeing Garfield High's JROTC drill team and was very impressed. I enjoyed the uniform and the feeling of belonging to something. In the three years of JROTC you are expected to go through the ranks as if you were in the army proper. I ended up as a cadet captain before graduating, which was good going for me.

During my first year at Garfield, Mom and Dad bought their first home in California, in Rosemead. It was a tract house built on the dry river bed of the San Gabriel River. This meant that I was to have to move to Rosemead High School. Our house was too far away to walk to school and a school bus was required to pick us up. The house was brand new and a source of great pride for Mom. She had achieved the American dream.

Rosemead High reminded me somewhat of Montebello. The culture at Rosemead was very different from Garfield. Rosemead's cultural dress code was Levi jeans, white tee-shirt and – if in a club – a very cool club jacket. The jacket that I thought was extremely cool was that worn by "the Aristocrats". For the first time, I was able to chat with a girl, and felt that this was great progress since I always put the female part of humanity on a pedestal. From my new female friend, I learned that the most-liked boys in school were the jocks. Knowing that I could not make the football team, I thought it would be good to try and get into one of the clubs.

One of the school troublemakers, who was a member of the Aristocrats, told me that he could get me into the Aristocrats if I would fight one of the jocks. The jock that he had in mind was an Aristocrat and not as bad as he was for picking on people, but still was not averse to having a go at someone. I was to start the fight in front of the school while waiting for the bus.

As we stood in line for the bus the troublemaker signaled that I should start. By now I had decided that this was not such a great idea but the desire to join the Aristocrats was stronger than my judgment. With a great adrenalin rush I approached the jock and said he was a bastard for picking on me and threw a blow to the middle of his chest. He then started to take off his jacket and time slowed down. Luckily, the boys' vice-principal who was in front of the school at the time, trying to keep order, had witnessed the whole thing. We were both taken off to his office and questioned. He suggested that we get the permission of our parents and meet in the gym behind closed doors and finish it like gentlemen in a boxing ring. I had reservations about this, since judgment was returning, and also after seeing the size of my opponent. It all sounded like "going to the toilet to finish it at Griffith."

I was given a deserved two-week suspension, which did not please my parents. During the two weeks off, I approached Garfield about returning and to my surprise was allowed to return with permission from Rosemead High. It meant a long commute but at least I would be with a culture and pecking order that I understood. The arrangement was that I was to ride in with Dad in the morning and return with him in the evening. I was living in the suburbs but going to school in town.

CHAPTER EIGHT

GARFIELD DAYS

LATER in the first year of high school, my family bought and moved to a house at 13620 Hutchcroft Street in a suburb development in La Puente, California. Mom and Dad had sold the new house that they had bought in Rosemead and bought this resale property. I'm not sure exactly what happened but I think that the family made a profit on the Rosemead house since it was so new. I did not attempt to go to the local high school after the experience at Rosemead High. This meant that I had a longer commute as I was now some sixteen miles from Garfield. The former arrangement with Dad would not work since he was going to work on a different route now. In the mornings I would catch a lift from one of the new neighbors, who worked in Los Angeles, which meant I arrived at school early. In the evenings I usually hitchhiked home. Mom and Dad stayed in this house for many years but by now I just wanted to escape the chaos of home life.

The tenth grade at Garfield ended reasonably well and I managed the commuting. Sometimes when I hitchhiked home from school I would be wearing my Junior Reserve Officers' Training Corps uniform and some people thought that I was in the military and offered me a lift. They were surprised to find out that I was only a fifteen-year-old high school student.

The summer of 1960 was an exciting one; I was turning sixteen on 18 June and I could finally do what most every boy in America dreams of – drive a car. We were in a presidential election year and John F. Kennedy was running against Richard Nixon for the presidency. The presidential debate was very hot. It was not to be a normal routine summer. I took two summer school classes to make up for my failures and otherwise had a quiet time. I did little else but sleep for most of the time that I was not in a summer school class.

I had taken the written test for my learner's driving permit six months earlier. This permitted me to drive with a licensed driver over the age of eighteen while learning how to drive. Normally, parents would teach their children to drive but unfortunately Dad was not keen on teaching me.

During the summer of 1960, my uncle Sam visited us from Mobile. He had driven out to California and spent a little over a week with us. Uncle Sam was like my big brother and sensed the desire I had to drive. He had invited me to go back to Mobile to spend the remaining month of the summer vacation with him. On the trip back to Mobile, he let me drive his manual shift Ford part of the time, giving me instructions on how to drive along the way. When in Mobile he continued to give me driving instruction and took me to the licensing authorities to try and get an Alabama driver's license. Since he was not my legal guardian they refused. It was a blow not being able to get the license, but I will always be grateful to my uncle Sam for his efforts.

The month in Mobile was great. I always loved being with my uncle Sam. Uncle Sam still had not given up his music and he belonged to a band that played part-time at Brookley Air Force Base on the weekends. He would sometimes take me to his gigs at the non-commissioned officers' (NCO) club and I would sit at the bar and listen to his band play. I was introduced to alcohol while attending these outings. Sometimes, I would sneak an occasional Tom Collins, which the bartender would sell to me.

Uncle Sam and Aunt Sid had family friends who lived on the edge of Mobile Bay and whom we visited several times. They had a daughter of fifteen whom I thought at the time was very cute. We would swim together at the edge of Mobile Bay. On one occasion in the car going to visit, Aunt Sid noticed that I had borrowed some of Uncle Sam's aftershave lotion and she made a kidding remark about how good I smelled. Life with Uncle Sam and Aunt Sid was so different from California and I hated to see summer end. I took the Greyhound bus back to LA at the end of summer.

To my surprise, not long after I got back to California, Dad took me down to take my driver's test in his Ford station wagon. I passed the test, so the efforts of Uncle Sam were not wasted. However, I was not allowed to drive since the cost of insurance for a sixteen-year-old was too high. This was very frustrating but I had no other choice. In California, if you did not have a car, then the girls were not interested in you. Cars and drive-in movies were where much exploration between boys and girls went on. So without access to a car, there was much less of a chance to have a relationship with a girl.

The school year started in September 1960. However, the previous year, before being admitted to Garfield, we were all given the opportunity to determine our major. If students felt that they did not have any academic potential they would select one of the vocational streams such as auto mechanics or business. Initially, when starting at Garfield, guided by one of our advisors, I selected the academic stream, which meant that I was to study with the objective of attending university. Academic majors needed to have mathematics up to and including calculus, English, and a foreign language. My home environment and my study habits were not conducive for any stream that required after-school class work, and the academic stream was the most demanding on homework.

There were five kids at home with no supervision, as both Mom and Dad went to work during the day and when they got home they were too tired to be bothered with any of us. Since Dad had only a third grade education anyway, he would not have been much help. Dad always called me the "professor" in a sarcastic way, envious of where I had gotten to in my schooling. In the house, we had to fend for ourselves and a discipline for homework was not a virtue that was present. We would have the occasional family meal together but more often than not we would get our own dinners. I had developed a habit of bringing my books home from school only to put them down and pick them up again the next day to take back, as if I was using them for weight training.

In the tenth grade, I chose French as my foreign language, as Grandma had always bragged about her French background. Looking back, I should have considered Spanish since I was in a Mexican neighborhood and was surrounded by Spanish speakers. At sixteen, I simply did not have the discipline to put in the hours required to learn a language. The teacher was a bit of a clown as well; I remember him standing at the classroom door and opening it saying "ouvrez la porte," and then closing the door saying "fermez la porte." All the students in the class laughed at the manner in which he did this little performance. I guess the method worked because I remember the words till this day. However, just learning how to say "open the door" and "close the door" was not enough to earn a pass in French.

On the other hand, I found that I could learn enough algebra in class not to need to do homework. The teacher had told us that whatever grade we achieved in our final examination was to be our final grade. I learned that this was only encouraging talk since I received a B for my final exam but the teacher gave me an overall C grade. When I asked her about the discrepancy between what was told us at the start of the term and my final grade, she said that I was an exception since I had not handed in any homework at all. I felt cheated but did not challenge the teacher.

Besides French, I failed enough other classes in my first year at Garfield to be asked if I wished to change majors. My first year's grades had ruined my chances of getting accepted by a university and I wanted to start the second year with the objective only of finishing high school. I agreed and decided on business for my junior year of high school. I started my second year at Garfield as a business major but soon found that the classes also required a reasonable amount of homework to keep up with the material. Also, I found topics like accounting extremely boring. It looked like I was going to have a hard time getting through my high school diploma.

I was taking a keener interest in JROTC than most of my other classes; I found that I could function well there and had made a great circle of JROTC friends. Perhaps it provided the disciplined environment that was so lacking at home where I missed the structure of Grandma and Papa's house. The JROTC required a larger amount of structured discipline than my other classes but did not demand homework. In JROTC we had to learn close-order-drill and a little history of the US Army (as the US Army tells it), US Army military organization, etc. It was not that my other school classes did not require discipline, it was just a different type of discipline; other classes required self-discipline to do homework as an individual, whereas JROTC demanded more of an overt discipline that was easier to understand.

I remember a teenage conversation with my JROTC friends as we were sitting in the JROTC building next to the physical education complex. I recall that one of the topics was Cuba. I had stated that it would be great to go as a mercenary and fight to free Cuba from communism. Then one of my Mexican friends countered by saying that he would prefer to fight in a coup to free Mexico from its poverty. We were both teenagers without a great deal of worldly knowledge but had strong views of where we should put our military efforts. It surprised me that someone would prefer to fight in Mexico rather than want to fight communism. Now looking back, I understand that my friend was a product of a culture that was different from mine even though we were both in the same country and school. We had a lot in common, but yet a lot of differences.

A major highlight of the beginning of the eleventh grade was the visit of J.F. Kennedy to East Los Angeles College on 1 November 1960, just one week before the presidential election. As local JROTC cadets, we were sent to the grounds of the East Los Angeles Junior College's sports stadium to stand guard at various points as the entourage arrived. It was an impressive experience, since support for Kennedy had filled the stadium. After the event got started we were released from our posts and allowed to move around on the field before reassuming our positions just before the entourage left. I was able to get close to the sitting area and managed to get the autographs of Frank Sinatra, Janet Leigh and Milton Berle, who had all came out to support the Kennedy campaign effort. All three of these entertainers were well known at the time and I felt an air of excitement. It would have been enough to hear Kennedy speak live, let alone get to see in person people of such celebrity status and get their autographs. JFK was elected president in November 1960.

The second year business major turned out to be almost as disastrous as the academic major since it required homework. Not as much homework as the academic major but enough to cause my grades to suffer. I was also experimenting with other classes and took an aviation course. Besides JROTC, this was my favorite course of the second year but it was only an elective course. We learned the theory of flying and flight navigation. In the course, we were set one practical problem where we had to do a flight plan and fly in a small four-place (four seats) Cessna and guide the chartered pilot around LA. I really loved this course and the navigation practical was very exciting. On the navigation practical I sat in the four-place Cessna with three other students and each of us had to navigate a leg in the flight plan using visual markers.

~~

On Friday, 20 January 1961, President Kennedy was sworn in. His inaugural address dominated television that evening and was to become a classic speech. We were all motivated by his famous line: "And so, my fellow Americans: ask not what your country can do for you – ask what you can do for your country." These were powerful words spoken in a time of transition during an overpowering Cold War. We were entering a new era and our president was calling on us not to be selfish but to try and work toward the good of our country and indeed the good of mankind.

Garfield had a large auditorium and had to have students to shift the equipment during assemblies, plays and other events that took place during the year. In the second year I joined the stage crew since I enjoyed moving the equipment and being part of the excitement of the production of the various events. Being part of a team that put on productions provided good teamwork experience. It also meant that I often had to stay after school to rehearse for the various productions. I enjoyed the rehearsals since they gave me a feeling of working towards something as part of a group and a warm sense of belonging.

During the final part of the second year of high school, I received some shocking news. My mother's work finished early enough that day for her to offer me a ride, which saved me from having to hitchhike home. As we were walking to the car she told me she was pregnant again. She told me she did not know how to tell Dad. I stood there in disbelief for a moment, as the reality of what I had just been told sank in. As she drove home it was apparent that she was not pleased. This was her seventh child and she was in her late thirties. It seemed that my parents had a lot of children and never used birth control. I truly felt sorry for her. However, there was nothing I could do.

~~

On 25 May 1961, President Kennedy stood in front of a joint session of Congress and gave what became known as the "Man on the moon" speech. In this speech he stated:

> I believe that this nation should commit itself to achieving the goal, before this decade is out, of landing a man on the moon and returning him safely to the earth. No single space project in this period will be more impressive to mankind, or more important for the long-range exploration of space; and none will be so difficult or expensive to accomplish.

President Kennedy was asking Congress for funding for this great adventure. To those of us in high school this seemed like a great objective.

~~

The second year ended okay at Garfield but by now I'd failed so many classes that I would not be able to graduate with my class by just going to regular school. If I was going to graduate, I would have to take additional courses. I desperately wanted to get away from home and now that I was seventeen, I could go into the military if I had my parents' consent. I had gone to a US Army recruiter with a couple of my JROTC friends who had already decided to join the army. A seventeen-year-old is no match for the persuasiveness of a recruiter. He had given all of us the necessary documentation to have our parents sign us into active duty. I went home and asked Mom and Dad to sign the papers. It ended in a real argument and I finished up in tears as my escape plan did not work. To my dad's credit, he did not care if I went into the military or not, but he insisted that I finish high school first.

During that summer, Dad got me a job with the steel construction company that he was working in part-time as a layout man. I was supposed to be eighteen to work in steel construction but I had lied about my age to get the job. Dad had originally told the foreman that I was eighteen and I was instructed by Dad to confirm this when asked. The age issue was never again brought up. As a layout man, Dad would take the blueprints and mark out where holes were to be drilled on the steel beams. I was just a general worker and together we would pre-drill the holes and prepare the steel so that when we went to the building site we just bolted the beams together. I found the work very tiring but it paid well. My hands got extremely callused by the steel. I would often work more than just eight hours a day and the overtime pay was very good.

Dad once laid out the steel for an apartment building and had drilled some of the holes in the wrong place. Since he was my dad I had to take a magnetic drill press and drill a lot of the holes in the proper place. This was done on the second storey of the steel frame for the apartment and I soon got used to walking the beams at a height.

By the end of summer I had accumulated enough money to buy a motorcycle. I bought a secondhand Allstate 125 cc, a machine made by the Austrian company, Puch. It was not a Harley but I could get the bike up to 80 miles per hour and loved riding it. It was to serve me well in the last year of high school and I no longer had to hitchhike back and forth to classes.

During the final year of high school the prom took place but I did not attend. I did not know a girl well enough to ask her to the event. Also, I was not sure that my mom and dad would pay the expenses. Since I only had a motorcycle and no chance of using Dad's car I figured I would be embarrassed if I asked a girl to the prom and she accepted the invitation and then I would not be able to get her there.

To graduate with my class I needed to make up some credits for the fail grades that I'd had in the previous two years. I was able to take some credit adult education courses at El Monte High School. I found the atmosphere in adult education a little better. Regular day high school was not good since many students were there, not because they wished to be, but because their parents had insisted that they go. The group that I met was from the San Gabriel Valley also, but they were out of school and now wished to finish. One other person, Rick, was – like me – trying to make up classes. We befriended each other and kept in contact till I left the Marines.

My brother David was born in December of the final year of high school. There is more than seventeen years' difference between my brother David and myself. David was only six months old when I left for basic training, so I never really knew him. His arrival was a shock to the family as we were now six kids, and the new baby drew more than his share of attention.

A good friend from Garfield, John Chavez, always wanted to be in the Marines. He had a lot of knowledge about the Pacific War and the part the US Marine Corps had played in the Pacific campaigns; he even had a souvenir Japanese sword. We visited the local US Marines recruiter on Whittier Boulevard and were soon talked into a program where we could do some of our inactive reserve duty prior to going on active duty. We would enlist in May and go on active duty in August. The three months before training were to count toward the standard six-year contract of four years active duty and two years inactive duty. This seemed to be a good idea at the time and I persuaded Mom and Dad to sign a parental consent since I would not be eighteen till June. Dad was disappointed that I had not followed him in joining the US Navy but signed anyway. We both went down and took the pre-enlistment tests and physical. I passed and John failed. I was now an official US Marine recruit but would miss not having John with me.

As we approached the end of the last year of high school I had made up the needed credits to graduate with my class; I had done this by attending summer school after year 10 and night school in year 12. Preparation was underway for the all-night party after the graduation ceremony. Again, I was not in the in-crowd and so did not attend the party. I had to borrow a suit from Papa who had moved to California during my final year of high school. I was now six feet four inches tall and only Papa's suit would fit. Grandma and Papa had sold the house in Gulfport before moving to California.

The graduation ceremony took place in the stadium at East Los Angeles College and I was one of several hundred graduates who crossed the stage to receive a high school diploma in June 1962. We were lost in a crowd – parents hearing only the name of their child in the procession – as we filed by and were presented with our diplomas.

CHAPTER NINE

LEAVING HOME FOR MARINE CORPS BOOT CAMP

AFTER graduation and my eighteenth birthday in 1962, I was planning on enjoying a good summer before going on active duty in August. On 26 June, we were all having a meal together at home and as usual my dad started after me about whether I was going to look for a job or was I going to lie around the house sponging off the family. I said I was going on active duty in just two months and wanted to relax a little. The discussion turned into a heated argument and it ended up with me in tears and my sister Sue shouting at him: "Leave him alone." For Sue it was too much; even if we did not get along that well she felt for me. I got up and went directly to bed. It was still early and I was in tears; I felt ashamed since I was now eighteen and could still cry easily. While lying in bed thinking about what I should do, I decided to report for active duty the next day.

Before sunrise the next morning, I got up and packed my belongings in accordance with the list given to me by the recruiter. I only needed a few items, such as a couple of changes of underwear, my toiletries, etc., since I was going to have to be issued with military clothing. I also took the papers that I needed to be inducted into the Marines. I knew if Mom found out she would talk me out of going until August. She seemed to want me to stay at home, perhaps from guilt at leaving me with Grandma and Papa all those years. Anyway, I'd made up my mind already.

At 6:00 am I took my bag and walked to our neighbor Norm's house; it was Norm who had given me a lift to high school for the past two and a half years. It was with a little sadness that I looked around at our house for the last time even if it had been hell for me. Norm was very punctual and always left at six and he agreed to drop me off close to the induction center. On the trip into Los Angeles, I told Norm that I had decided to go on active duty early as it was boring lying around the house. I lied because I did not wish to expose the internal squabbles of the family.

I found my way to the LA Armed Forces Induction Center from the information on the letter which had been given to me when I had taken the initial examination and battery of tests. The center processed all new inductees to the armed forces and I joined in the procedure with all the other inductees of the day. There was loads of paperwork to complete and another physical to undergo. It finally ended with all of us being sworn in together, no matter what service we were going into, by an army officer who was attached to the center. The oath I took was:

> I, Orville Leverne Clubb, do solemnly swear that I will support and defend the Constitution of the United States against all enemies, foreign and domestic; that I will bear true faith and allegiance to the same; and that I will obey the orders of the President of the United States and the orders of the officers appointed over me, according to regulations and the Uniform Code of Military Justice. So help me God.

It was a very solemn oath and every person who enters the armed forces has to take it. The oath over, we were divided into groups. I was put with five other new recruits for the Marines and we were to wait for transportation to take us to the Marine Corps Recruit Depot (MCRD) in San Diego, California.

I now felt it was safe to call Mom. I was already sworn in and she could not talk me into coming home. I found an empty telephone booth in a row of booths inside the facility and called home. Mom answered; I had obviously woken her up and she sounded groggy as she asked where I was. I said, "Mom, I was just sworn into the Marines!" She said, "Honey, your dad did not mean what he said. Come on home." I paused a moment, the message was not getting through. It was as always. Mom only heard what she wanted to hear. I then said, "Mom, listen carefully; I was just sworn in and I have to go since they are about to take us to boot camp. I could not come home even if I wanted to." Mom then dissolved into tears and I could her sobbing uncontrollably on the phone repeating: "Oh baby! Oh baby!" Hearing my mom cry started me crying in sympathy. Here I was, an eighteen-year-old about to go off to the Marine Corps boot camp, in a telephone booth at the induction center in uncontrollable tears – and this was for the second time in two days. I looked around to see if anyone was looking. I was in luck, everyone was doing their own thing and I was not noticed. I said, "I'm sorry, Mom, but I have to go." She said, "Honey, please take care. I love you." I said, "I love you too, Mom. Next time you see me, I'll be a marine. Bye." I hung up the phone and tried to clear the tears as best I could. I then saw that I was not the only one who'd had a tearful telephone call. The telephone booths were in the center for the very purpose of enabling inductees to make calls before being taken off for military training. Many of the young men emerging from the other phone booths were trying to hide tears as well.

I rejoined the Marine Corps group and we all sat patiently for nearly an hour. Finally, a marine in full khaki uniform came in and told us very brusquely to go out to a truck parked outside that had arrived with a driver to take us to the Recruit Depot. – We were now sworn in and there was no need to treat us nicely anymore. – The marine handling the paperwork here and taking us to the MCRD had a very different way of treating us than the marine recruiter or the Induction Center staff. He was rude and often swore, and began by saying something along the lines of: "You pricks, hurry up and get in the fucking truck, we haven't got all day." I soon learned that the word "fuck" was the most frequently used word in the Corps during boot camp and was used in most sentences uttered by drill instructors (DIs) and other marines dealing with us during training. He shouted at us: "You fucking turds had better be quiet back here; I don't want to hear any talking or see any smoking."

We loaded onto the back of an open truck that had wooden slatted seats down each side and a tarp over it. As we rode towards San Diego, we could see the scenery along the freeway out of the back of the truck. At times we could see the ocean, at other times the dry desert. The ride was more than two-and-a-half-hours long but we eventually arrived at the front gate of the MCRD in San Diego. As we pulled into the depot, I could see from the back of the truck new recruits policing up (cleaning) the grounds around the front gate. They were wearing bright yellow sweatshirts, with a big red Marine Corps emblem on the chest; they wore white tennis shoes on their feet and their pants were the standard green utility pants, as we called them in the Marines (the army calls them fatigues) and a utility cap. One of the recruits who was policing up looked at us coming in and just shook his head. All of us in the truck laughed nervously and one of the boys next to me said, "That is a bad sign."

The Recruit Depot was an impressive place with buildings that resembled a Spanish fort. The truck traveled around the MCRD until it arrived at the receiving barracks. We were met by several marine DIs who immediately started shouting at us to get off the truck fast and line up. Having quickly obeyed, we were told to stand at attention in shoe prints painted in yellow on the sidewalk. By doing this we looked a little like a military formation. I understood what was expected from my days in the Junior Reserve Officers' Training Corps but some of the other five recruits must never have had any military training and were drawing more than their share of attention. Drill instructors have a technique of putting their face about five inches from a recruit's face and shouting insults at the recruit at the top of their voice to intimidate him. When at attention we were always to look to the front. A new recruit made the mistake of looking toward the DI and I remember the first of a series of insults on that first day, which was: "What are you looking at, maggot?" The recruit answered, "Sir, nothing, sir." The DI got within his five inches of the face position and shouted: "Are you calling me nothing, turd?" Then he moved away and in a gentle voice said, "Do you like me boy?" – There was no winning answer to this question. If the recruit said no, then there was a lot of shouting about five inches from the recruit's face about "why don't you like me," etc. If the recruit said yes (which normally happened), he would get the standard line of questions, which would start with the DI saying, in a loud voice: "Liking leads to loving and loving leads to fucking; are you going to fuck me boy...?" This could go on for several minutes.

The receiving barracks was a staging facility for recruits and we would stay there until there were enough of us to form training platoons. Also, it was where we received our first instruction on how to become a member of the US Marine Corps. However, it did not count for the formal training of boot camp. As we stood at attention in front of the receiving barracks, we were given a quick summary of the rules by one of the DIs. We were told that we could not speak unless spoken to and we were never to speak to a fellow recruit. If we wanted to speak, we had to ask the person whom we wished to speak to for permission to speak. And we were only allowed to speak after permission was granted. The first and last word from our mouths would be "sir" if we said anything. So if we wished to speak we were to say, "Sir, permission to speak to the drill instructor, sir." When acknowledging that we understood an order we were to respond "aye aye, sir" and complete the order. We were then told to get on our hands and knees and pat the ground. We did so and one of the DIs said, "I want you to know that the fucking ground is the only thing lower than you till you prove yourself to be worthy of being called a marine." He continued, "Some of you are not going to make it. Until you prove yourselves worthy of being in my Marine Corps or we throw you out, the ground is the only thing lower than you; all of you are lower than whale shit!" We were then told that while in training we would be called "private" and would not be called a marine until graduating from boot camp. In reality, over the next couple of months we were called many things and normally only "private" in formal situations. I felt that these marine DIs (and others after them) were the most tyrannical, sadistic people that I had ever encountered. They made my dad look like a saint. It was beyond comprehension that a human being could treat another human being with so little regard for their feelings and self-esteem.

The first tasks at the receiving barracks were to usher us in and give us a high and tight haircut, then an initial issue, which included a bucket, scrub brush, laundry soap, our utility uniforms, a bright yellow sweatshirt, white tennis shoes, towels, soap, shoe polishing kit, boots, new military shoes, a combination lock and writing paper. Also, we were given a red Marine Corps manual, the *Guidebook for Marines*, which described the basics of being a marine. This was to be our reading for the MCRD training cycle. It was like a textbook for a university course. For the haircut, toiletries, shoe polish, combination lock, laundry soap, the *Guidebook for Marines*, etc., that we'd been given, we had to sign a chit so that the money to pay for these "non-military" issue items would come from our first month's pay.

After the initial issue we were ordered to change into the receiving barracks' uniform of yellow sweatshirt etc. that we had seen the recruits wearing as we entered the MCRD. We were then taken to an area behind the barracks where a collection of empty boxes was lined up and were told to put all our civilian clothing and non-marine items into the box in front of us. The only exceptions were that recruits who needed glasses could keep them and any smokers could keep their lighters and cigarettes, if they had them. We soon learned what the "smoking lamp" was. If the DI said the smoking lamp was lit, then smokers could light up and smoke till the DI said the lamp was out. When the smoking lamp was out, those recruits who were smoking would have to "field strip" the cigarette butt. Field strip meant to tear the cigarette paper open, drop the remaining tobacco on the ground, and pocket the paper and filter until the recruit could trash it properly. This was one of the few privileges afforded us and for those of us who did not smoke, it was an opportunity lost. Many recruits who were non-smokers took up the habit during basic training as it was seen as a valued privilege.

After we'd packed our civilian belongings into a box, we had to write a letter home. On a large board in big letters, posted where we could all see, there was a draft of what we were to copy home to our parents. The content of the letter was to be copied directly word for word; the only difference being the name we signed it with. The letter basically said: "I have arrived at the MCRD safely, I am fine and here are all my civilian things since I will not need them during training. Love to the family." Each letter was read to make sure that we had written what we were supposed to say. We then put the letter into the box and sealed it. The box was taken away and mailed home at our expense.

We were then taken back inside the receiving barracks to a squad bay that was to be our home during receiving. By now I thought I had arrived in hell; I was in a state of complete disorientation and my mind was going through such mental trauma that I secretly longed to be home. We were each assigned a bunk bed and issued with a set of bed linen and a wall locker. We were then told to open our assigned wall locker and stand at attention in front of it with all our new items. We were made to strip naked and were sent for a shower in a large common shower room under the watchful eye of the receiving barracks DIs. After a fast shower and drying ourselves quickly we were rushed back to our wall lockers and bunks. We were then instructed to get back into our receiving uniform. After we'd all dressed quickly in our utility pants, tee-shirt, yellow sweatshirt, etc., the DI told us that we had thirty seconds to get everything except our bed linen into the wall locker and lock it with the combination lock. He then started to count from thirty backwards: "...29, 28, 27..." I struggled and tried to open the combination lock with the combination number given, but I could not open it. By the time he'd finished the countdown and shouted, "...1, time's up; ATTENTION," everyone had finished and locked their wall lockers and was at attention except me. The DI looked at me and said, "What the fuck is wrong with you, maggot?" I started to say, "The combin...," when the DI shouted, "What is the first and last word from your fucking mouth, turd?" I then shouted, "Sir, the combination lock does not work, sir." He slowly walked over and took the lock and the combination attached from me while I stood at attention. He continued to walk over to a table a few feet from me, sat down and casually tried the lock, which opened for him on the first try. He stared at me and did not do or say anything for what seemed like an eternity. I felt the terror of being singled out. He then threw the lock, which missed me and hit my wall locker behind me and fell on the floor. He shouted: "Pick up the fucking lock and lock your wall locker, shithead." I shouted: "Sir, aye aye, sir." I picked up the lock and locked the locker and returned to attention. To my surprise that was the end of it; I guess they had too much to cover in the first day to single me out further.

 We were then told how to make up our bunk beds Marine Corps style. We had two sheets, a pillow, a pillowcase and two blankets. The DI showed us how to make the bunk up correctly with the two sheets and blanket, by making hospital corners, positioning the pillow and then the second blanket covering the pillow. We were shown that if made up correctly a coin dropped onto the center of the bunk would bounce. The DI demonstrated this with a twenty-five-cent coin. We each made up our bunks as closely as possible to the instructions given. We were to get a new sheet and pillowcase once a week. The top sheet from the previous week was to become the bottom sheet. And the old bottom sheet and old pillowcase were to be sent to the laundry.

 After this, we were moved to a classroom for the initial indoctrination talk. The talk went over the instructions that were given to us upon first arriving and the training that was about to happen. We learned that we would be in the receiving facility till a training series of three platoons could be formed.

By now, it was late and the day seemed surreal, starting from leaving home in the morning, talking to my mother and then being in a place that would be incomprehensible to most humans on this Earth. After an afternoon of indoctrination it was time for evening chow. I had not had anything to eat all day and was looking forward to food. The DI tried to teach us a little close-order drill on our way to the mess hall, but many of the recruits were untrained and we basically meandered to the mess hall. Once there we were instructed on how to take a stainless steel tray and our eating utensils, stand at attention and side step through the mess line accepting what was given to us in the tray's compartment. When we got to the table we were instructed to place our trays on the table and stand at attention in front of the bench that was used for sitting. We were reminded to eat without talking to each other. We were to stand at attention until the DI ordered us "ready seats." After this instruction the DI said, "Ready seats." We were sitting at attention when he said, "That was fucking awful; we do it again, girls, till we get it right." We went through the procedure several times till the DI said, "I guess that will have to do for now; you maggots had better start getting squared away." He said, "At ease," which was the signal to relax and start eating and he walked away.

It must not have been more than three minutes later when I noticed the table rising and falling with a great thud. I turned to see that the DI had picked up one end of the table and dropped it to get our attention. He shouted, "What the fuck is wrong with you turds? Do you think you are eating in a fucking resort hotel or something? You should be finished by now; get your skuzzy asses outside and line up." In haste, we had to put our trays and eating utensils in the collection area and rush outside having not had much to eat.

The day at the receiving barracks finally ended and we were sent to our bunks to sleep. I was very hungry and lay there thinking that this was not what I had expected. I was wondering whether I could take nearly three months of this. However, in my mind I was determined to see it through; I was not going back to hear my father ridicule me for not being able to make it.

After a few days we were given a medical checkup along with a group of other recruits in receiving. We were getting close now to having enough recruits to form training platoons. We were only wearing our skivvies (military boxer-short underpants) and were forced to line up as they said in those days "assholes to bellybuttons." The receiving barracks medical was a totally humiliating experience where each of us had a big number written on the right side of our chest with a marker pen. We had no identity in this medical except the number on our chest. We had to stand at attention throughout the process. We were examined as a mass of flesh, our only distinction being our number. We had to move from one station to another and at each a US Navy doctor or corpsman would check for a specific physical thing as if it was an assembly line. I learned that I had a scoliosis when a navy corpsman walked up behind me at one of the stations and ran his hand over my spine and told the note-taking corpsman his finding about the slight curve in my back. It did not keep me out of the Corps in the initial medical during the recruitment process nor was it enough to send me home now.

We went through a hearing test, a series of inoculations (the shots were given using a high-pressure air gun to inject the vaccines) and there were lots of daily routines to keep us busy until training platoons could be formed.

Finally, I was put into Platoon 144. Our training series was Platoons 143, 144 and 145. The three training platoons would go through the training cycle together and compete with each other throughout the process. Training was to commence on 9 July 1966 and would continue to graduation on 18 September 1966.

CHAPTER TEN

STARTING BOOT CAMP

BOOT camp for US Marines in 1962 consisted of a number of informal and formal parts. The initial formal training at the Marine Corps Recruit Depot was a ten-week cycle which included one week of mess duty. The second formal part comprised four weeks with the Infantry Training Regiment (ITR) at Camp Pendleton. If you excluded the week of mess duty at the MCRD, then the formal training was thirteen weeks in length. In reality, the time spent in boot camp was longer because of having to do mess duty at the MCRD and possible extra mess or guard duty before going to the ITR. A recruit could spend up to twenty weeks in boot camp. The thirteen weeks of formal training in 1962 gave the Marines the longest training cycle of any of the US armed services.

For Platoon 144, the MCRD boot camp started on Monday, 9 July 1962. Our uniform was changed to reflect that we had left the receiving barracks. As we moved to our training platoon area we gave up the bright yellow sweatshirt with utility pants, white tennis shoes and utility cap, in favor of a standard set of utilities that we would wear throughout our time of active duty. The only difference was that our pants were worn without blousing the boots (using a garter-like piece of elastic to hitch up the leg) so that nothing could crawl up the pant leg in the field. Our utility shirt was buttoned up to the top button. These two irregularities in the way we wore our utility uniforms were to be changed to the standard style as we progressed through training. At the MCRD you could look at how the utility uniform was worn by recruits and determine at what general stage of boot camp they were. First the bright yellow sweatshirt of receiving was worn. Then, once a recruit had made it through to marksmanship training, he would have his boots bloused. If he had an open collar then this meant he had completed initial basic training and was about to be shipped to the ITR, where a recruit was formally called "marine" instead of "private."

Before leaving the receiving barracks for our new boot camp platoon we were issued with M14 rifles; we were some of the first US Marine recruits to be trained with the M14. We were told we had to memorize our rifle's serial number. The serial number would be asked in rifle inspections. The M14 was an attempt to standardize ammunition for weapons with NATO at a time when all NATO countries used the same 7.62 mm caliber round. We still talked of feet and yards in 1962 but found this very inconvenient when doing joint operations with NATO allies. The M14 had been part of the US Army since 1959 but only in 1962 was it being used as the standard rifle in the Fleet Marine Force (FMF). The M14 had a lot of similarities to the M1 rifle that I had used in the Junior Reserve Officers' Training Corps but had a magazine, which meant that it could take up to twenty rounds instead of the eight-round clip of the M1 rifle. Also, the M14 rifle was lighter and it had a selector that would allow the rifle to be fired either semi-automatically or fully automatically.

Our rifle was to be our constant companion throughout boot camp and active duty with the Marines. The rifle is the tool of trade and every marine, no matter what his military occupation specialty (MOS), had to be proficient at using this tool. When on active duty, every marine must qualify on the standard Marine Corps rifle range at least once a year. In the 1960s, a marine was required to fire from 100 yards, 300 yards and 500 yards at standard marksmanship targets.

We were marched from the receiving barracks to the platoon area with our new possessions, which included our sea bag with the initial uniform issue, bucket and new rifle. The platoon areas were made up of Quonset huts. The area in front and between each hut was planted in ice plant, which we learned to hate. The drill instructors would always make us water the ice plant and rake the "grass." There was no real grass there, but if the DI said there was grass, we took care of the "grass." The MCRD was next to the ocean and the ground was sandy. With a rake we used to make nice neat rows in the sand surrounding the Quonset huts not covered by ice plant. The DI would get after the platoon if he ever found a footprint on his "grass" and we would have to ceremoniously "rake the grass" to the DI's standard.

Inside the Quonset huts was a squad bay that was filled with bunk beds. The bunk bed was referred to as a "rack" and, with our wall locker and foot locker, was to be our only piece of real estate for the period of time that we did our MCRD training.

The Quonset huts that the platoon occupied opened on to what we referred to as "the road." The platoon DIs had an office in the middle in one of the Quonset huts which was manned 24 hours a day by duty DIs. The road was a paved pathway that ran through the rows of Quonset huts. It was where we would get our platoon into formation when the DIs were ready to deal with us. When we heard "144 on the road" from a DI we only had a few seconds to get in platoon formation and stand at attention on the road.

Having been taken to our new Quonset hut and assigned our racks, I needed to go to the toilet. I went to the door of the hut and saw one of our junior DIs, Corporal Miller. Corporal Miller was unusual in that he was an African-American and our only black DI in the training series. I shouted, "Sir, the private requests permission to go to the head, sir." Corporal Miller looked at me and said, "Get back inside, shithead." I shouted, "Sir, aye aye, sir," did a formal about face and started to walk back toward my rack. When I heard, "Hey you turd, come back here." I turned and went back to the door of the Quonset hut and stood at attention. He said, "Have you ever had any military training, maggot?" I shouted back, "Sir, yes sir; sir I had three years of JROTC in high school, sir." He then asked, "What is your name, private?" I replied, "Sir, Clubb, sir." He then said, "Get the fuck out of my sight." I shouted, "Sir, aye aye, sir." I went back to my rack and was under pressure to have a pee till we finally had a head break.

As a consequence of me showing off my knowledge of my days in the JROTC I found that I was a squad leader for a short time during the beginning of recruit training. I lost the position when it was found that I was physically very weak and had difficulty with the physical training. This was as a result of my using the JROTC to avoid doing physical education classes in high school. However, we had to learn a lot of the history of the Marines, structure of the Corps and do general military courses. The DIs would often place me with recruits who were having trouble with the classroom material and have me tutor them when we were sitting on our buckets on the road to shine our shoes or clean our rifles.

As part of our initial issue, we had a bucket. This was used for doing our laundry, since we were not allowed to use the base laundry until after several weeks of training. We had to wash all our clothes and towels by hand in our bucket in a laundry area that was at the end of the road next to our toilets and showers. We were told that in the field during combat we would not have a base laundry. The bucket became an essential tool that was to be used for other purposes besides washing. We used it for weight training by filling it with sand and as a seat to sit on in the road to shine our shoes, and at the same time, perhaps, deal with the rote learning of things like our eleven general orders. Every recruit had to memorize these orders and be able to recite them on demand. If while sitting on the bucket the DI shouted, "What is your second general order?" We would shout in reply in unison: "Sir, my second general order is: To walk my post in a military manner, keeping always on the alert and observing everything that takes place within sight or hearing, sir."

The road was where we had Mail Call, which signaled personnel to assemble for the distribution of mail, and the DIs would make general announcements to the training platoon. Mail Call was always looked forward to as we might hear from home. At the MCRD we were completely cut off and mail was a way of connecting with the outside world. We would "fall out" in platoon formation when the DI shouted, "Mail Call." After the platoon was formed we would do a close-order drill movement on the command of the DI called "open ranks" (the 1st squad took two steps forward, the 2nd squad took one step forward, the 3rd squad stood fast and the 4th squad took one step backward). Open ranks allows enough room between the rows of recruits to be able to walk in between the squads. When someone's name was called for an item of mail, the recruit had to shout, "Sir, here, sir," and run between the ranks, around to the front of the platoon, run by the DI, take the letter on the run, and then continue the run back to his place in the platoon and take his position once again.

The formal classroom training of the first week was made up of military history (as seen by the Marines) and use of the M14 rifle (how to disassemble/assemble the three main groups of the rifle, etc.), the meaning of our general orders, structure of the Corps, and so on. Also, during this first week we started on physical training. On our first day we had our first run as a platoon, which was for less than a mile. Sergeant Smallwood, one of our junior DIs, took us in platoon formation at double time (twice as fast as a regular march pace) through the streets of the MCRD. Even the fittest recruit had trouble with this run since it was the first time any of us had run in combat boots; it was like running with weights on our feet. As we came back into the platoon area and stood at attention on the road in platoon formation we could see that Sergeant Smallwood was not even in a sweat. The whole platoon on the other hand was sweating and huffing and puffing. At this moment, I wished that I had taken physical education classes instead of JROTC. We later learned that Sergeant Smallwood had left Force Recon (Reconnaissance) to become a DI. Sergeant Smallwood was in terrific physical shape. He addressed us on the road, saying, "You fucking girls are in worse shape than my grandma! You had better get with the fucking program or you will find yourself transferred to the motivation platoon till you are in shape! Very soon you will be doing five miles on each run and asking for more!"

The motivation platoon was bad news. It was for recruits who needed strengthening or to lose weight. If you went to the motivation platoon you dropped out of the training cycle and remained out of it until you could keep up with the physical training standards of the new training platoon to which you were assigned. The motivation platoon meant more time at the MCRD. If it took, say, one month to get into proper shape that meant you had an additional month in boot camp. If you were sent to the motivation platoon you had two canteens strapped to your utility belt, ran everywhere you went and did PT (sit-ups, push-ups, etc.) all day. Recruits who were overweight were supervised through the chow line in the mess hall to make sure that they dropped the extra weight. They ran and exercised from morning till night.

During this first phase of training we were taken to the depot swimming pool and tested on our ability to swim. It was important to identify the non-swimmers so that they could attend special classes and be taught. You were not allowed to graduate from boot camp till you could swim to a minimum standard. If I remember correctly it was twelve laps up and down the pool using at least two different strokes. I was luckily able to pass the swimming test. Those of us who passed were then taken to a tower that simulated the height of the side of a ship and taught how to jump off into water. We crossed our feet to make a good entry and crossed our arms with one hand holding our nose to keep the water out.

Before going to chow each evening we had to follow two daily rituals. The first was gym chin-ups. The style of chin-up in the strength training of the early 1960s was to pull yourself up with your hands holding the chin-up bar forward instead of backward. This prevents you from swinging your feet forward and making reaching the chin-up bar easier. It also works the forearms by using different muscles from those used for the traditional chin-up. I remember the first week of training and that the main reason for my losing the squad leader position was my inability to do many of this type of chin-up. You had to break from the previous chin-up by hanging with your arm muscles relaxed. It took considerably more strength to start each chin-up from the relaxed position. For a perfect score you needed to do eighteen chin-ups. On the night of our first chin-ups, our duty DI was Sergeant Yoder, who all of us recruits considered insane. He was someone that we could not read at all. He kept his military manner at all times. As I finished my first chin-up and could not get the second after breaking and hanging, I heard Sergeant Yoder shout, "You've got to be shitting me! You can't be that fucking weak! You look like a candidate for the motivation platoon! If you're going to stay with this fucking platoon you had best get some strength!" I shouted, "Sir, aye aye, sir," and went to the second part of the daily routine.

Going back to my rack I got my toiletry kit and towel and set off to do the second of the daily rituals, the three Ss: "shit, shower and shave." It was a routine that we had to follow each day of boot camp at the MCRD. The platoon road was designed with the real road on one side of the rows of Quonset huts and the head (toilets) and the outdoor laundry area on the other. The laundry area was where twice a week we washed our dirty towels, skivvies and utilities on a large, flat, concrete slab that was table height and had water faucets, using our scrub brushes on the flat concrete, and rinsing our clothes in our buckets. The head had two sides; one side housed the toilets and urinals in a large open area, the other provided an open shower area with a large mirrored section with wash basins for shaving. Privacy was not an option as all the areas were open. The idea of the three Ss was that you would go to the head and take care of nature's call, then go to the shower room for your shower and finish with a shave. As we returned to our rack, the duty DI would inspect everyone to see if we had shaved properly. I had very few hairs on my face to shave since my beard did not grow fully until my early twenties. I was sent back the first time as I'd not considered my few small hairs worth shaving. Thereafter I shaved carefully.

On Sundays, we were divided up into groups based on our religion. In the early 1960s, these comprised three main groups, namely, Catholic, Protestant and Jewish. My recruiter had only been able to spell Baptist, but I was put in the Protestant group. We had no choice; we were called out by name for each group and marched to our religious service. After the service we were marched back to our platoon area and went to chow. The afternoon was spent sitting on our buckets working on the leather of our uniforms. Also, during this time we again recited our eleven general orders. In June 1962, we still had brown leather for our dress-uniform and had to spit-shine our shoes and the bill of our dress cap till they shone like a mirror. We had to saddle-soap our boots and were not allowed to spit-shine them. We were told that spit-shining sealed the leather, our feet would not be able to breathe and it would cause the boot-leather to crack.

During the early stage of boot camp we did a lot of bucket drill with sand to simulate weights. We could vary the weight of the bucket by the amount of sand that was added. When we needed to have two buckets we would work with another recruit and take turns using two buckets. We did a variety of exercises with buckets. It was a very efficient method of weight training.

Nights while at boot camp started when the duty DI would put us in our racks at 2100 hours when Taps (lights out) was bugled over the PA system. When lights went out we would sometimes try and break the taboo about speaking to each other. There would be a little chatter going on around the squad bay. However, the duty DI would normally burst through the door of the Quonset hut and correct our wayward ways. Sometimes the transgression required us to do PT – forcing all of us to get out of our racks and do push-ups. Reveille would be sounded through the PA system of the recruit area of the MCRD at 5:30 am and every recruit was expected to be fully dressed and standing at attention by his rack when the lights went on.

We had three major obstacle courses that had to be done before graduation. The first course had walls to jump and ditches to swing across on ropes, and the tops of telephone poles cut and set unevenly from a height of about one foot to six foot high to allow us to develop balance while running over them. The second of the courses was designed to start building coordination and strength and help us overcome our natural fear of heights. It was called the Confidence Course and was introduced prior to going to Camp Matthews for rifle training. It involved a series of high obstacle walls and cargo nets that made us climb to great heights to get over some of the obstacles. This was designed to give us confidence on the sides of ships when descending cargo nets to landing crafts. The final course was at the end of the ten-week cycle and was the Endurance Course, which required us to use a lot of upper body strength. You mostly had to use only your upper body to get through the course.

CHAPTER ELEVEN

CAMP MATTHEWS AND MARKSMANSHIP TRAINING

IN 1962, the Marines put a great emphasis on marksmanship. It was important to be able to use a rifle effectively. At that time, recruits at the Marine Corps Recruit Depot received their marksmanship training at Camp Matthews near La Jolla, California. The training was at standard rifle targets with an emphasis on accuracy.

During its life, over a million marine recruits as well as other shooters received their marksmanship training at Camp Matthews. Camp Matthews was a United States Marine Corps military base from 1917 until 1964, when the base was decommissioned and transferred to the University of California to be part of the University of California, San Diego campus. In 1942, the base was officially named Camp Calvin B. Matthews. It was named after Brigadier General Matthews, who was a famous marine marksman of the 1930s, and the official naming took place on 23 March 1942. Up until 1942, it had simply been known as the Marine Rifle Range, La Jolla. At its height, Camp Matthews contained at least fifteen different shooting ranges as well as various buildings and other infrastructure. The facilities at Camp Matthews included seven barracks, approximately 270 tents, administration buildings, quartermaster storerooms, magazines, an armory, maintenance shops, a dispensary, a service station and a main post exchange. The shooting facilities included six rifle ranges, one pistol range, one mortar/flame thrower cum hand-grenade court cum bazooka range (Range H), three small bore ranges, one skeet range and three school ranges (non-shooting practice ranges).

For us in 1962, this part of our training cycle started with a hike from the MCRD to Camp Matthews. We were allowed to blouse our boots, which marked an advance in our recruit training. Also, it was better to have boots bloused when hiking. As we arrived at the Camp, each of us was assigned to one of the tents. We had a folding cot as a rack. The tents had a raised wooden floor for a base, making them level, semi-permanent structures. We stored our packs on the racks during the day and put them under the racks at night. We had not taken our full issue for marksmanship training so we did not have a foot or wall locker. The tents were arranged similarly to the Quonset huts at the MCRD with a road in the center of the rows of tents. However, the tents were smaller and much closer together. In front of the tents we had ice plants and "grass," the same as the MCRD Quonset huts. We were issued a shooting jacket that had pads on the elbows as we were going to be using our elbows on the ground a lot.

We started our marksmanship training with formal classes explaining how to sight the rifle, the effects of the wind, etc. We learned rules such as the elevation rule – one click of the sight's elevation knob moves the strike of the bullet one inch for every 100 yards of the target's distance. We had not yet changed to the metric system since that would mean a complete overhauling of ranges and materials that had been tried and found true for many years with the Corps.

Camp Matthews provided a very complete education on the principles of formal marksmanship using standard targets. It was a good grounding on how to shoot your rifle and what you needed to do to hit what you were aiming at. We were told, as we started our marksmanship training, that the ability to shoot accurately was one of the reasons the US Marines earned the name Devil Dogs from the German Army in WWI. Marines could shoot and hit German troops from 1,000 yards. In the history of the Marine Corps classes we were told that a message was sent from the German front line at The Battle of Belleau Wood to their higher headquarters, describing the fighting abilities of the new, fresh, American Marines as "fighting like hounds from hell." Personally, I believe the title Devil Dogs was earned from more than just marksmanship.

We learned how to use the rear circle military sight, which was different from the open sights on a civilian rifle. You would image a crosshair in the circle and float the target on the centered front sight. We undertook a lot of formal theory and exercises before starting to do live firing. We went from theory to practice using a form of simulation such as sighting exercises. We needed to be sure that we could apply the theory to the rifle, and shooting accurately takes much practice. We would sight the rifle and another recruit would sit on a box with a target and we would have to try and "hit the bull's-eye."

After sighting exercises we went to what we called "strapping in." We learned the firing positions: prone (lying on the ground on our stomach), sitting, kneeling and off hand (standing). We practiced the firing positions over and over till they were second nature. We had to get into the positions correctly to make sure that the rifle would be steady and it required us sometimes to stretch and use muscles that we were not used to using. The drill instructors would observe the position that we took and come by and correct us if necessary. As with martial arts, where routines are practiced over and over again until they become part of muscle memory and you do not have to think about them, so it was with rifle training. We learned how to use the rifle strap to steady the rifle. Also, we learned to put the outside of the thumb of our right hand (or our left hand if firing left handed) onto the same place on our right cheek (or left cheek if firing left handed) each time, to ensure that we were holding the rifle the same way for each shot.

During this first week at Camp Matthews we got to fire an M14 in full automatic mode. Also, we were introduced to the .45 pistol and learned how to fire it. However, we did not fire for qualification with the .45. I found that I had a natural talent with the .45. It was a great experience firing it since I had only fired rifles up to that time.

After nearly a week of non-live firing, practicing sighting and snapping in with our M14, on the Friday we finally got to fire the rifle. The first day of practice firing came and we were divided into two groups. One group would fire and the other group would work the butts. For the group that was firing there were two recruits assigned per target: one recruit would fire while the other would record, then they would switch and the one that was recording would get to fire. Each firing session was ten rounds for a score of 100 points. The bull's-eye was worth ten points and the first circle was nine, the second was eight, and so on.

The butts were a deep trench with targets that were raised and lowered on a rail device. The man in the butts would stand and wait for the shot to take place. You could tell when the bullet hit the target by the loud pop sound. You would lower the target and mark the shot. The recruits in the butts were assigned in pairs to a target since it was difficult for one person alone to pull the target up and down. After the target was hit, the recruits in the butt would pull the target down and one recruit would mark where the shot had hit with a circular disk about two inches across that fitted into the hole made by the bullet (there were white disks for the black area and black disks for the white area) so that the person shooting could see his last shot and adjust his sights if necessary. The target would be raised and the other recruit, would hold a twenty-inch disk on a pole over the place the bullet hit so that the shooter and recorder could see where he had hit. When one firing session was finished, the target would be pulled down and the hole patched with what were known as "lick-em and stick-em" stickers, so that the previous bullet holes could not be seen for the next firing session. If the recruit missed the target, then "Maggie's drawers" were shown by waving a red flag across the front of the target from the left to the right. This was a big embarrassment and would be seen across the range.

On this first day of live fire we were finding out our "dope" (the sight settings for that position and distance) for the rifle, so we did not have a timed rapid fire but worked on our dope from that position. The whole purpose of the first day of live firing was to sight in the rifle. We had to fire and record our dope in a little record book we carried during live marksmanship training and fired from 100 yards, 300 yards and 500 yards with a variety of positions we learned while snapping in. When firing at 100 yards, we fired ten rounds off hand (standing) at a standard target, and a timed ten-round rapid fire using a sitting position at a target (called a D target) that had a silhouette shaped like a human body. We moved to the 300-yard firing line and worked on the dope for the kneeling position at a standard target and on the dope for the prone position for rapid fire at a silhouette target. We then moved to the 500-yard firing line and sighted in for the prone position at a standard target. At 500 yards, some recruits could not see the twenty-inch bull's eye so they had to sight in on the large number board in front of the butts marking their target. Also at 500 yards, wind was a critical factor in the shot. We would have to watch the flags on either end of the range to see if there was wind when we fired a shot. If, as we started to squeeze off the shot, the wind picked up with a gust, we would let go and wait for the wind to drop before attempting the shot. After finishing firing we went to noon chow. In the afternoon we swapped positions. The firing group pulled butts for the butts group of the morning.

We were allowed to receive visitors at the weekend and on the weekend at Camp Matthews my mother and the whole family came down including Grandma and Papa. We were only allowed an hour together and we met in a designated visitors' area that had picnic tables. I was very happy to be visited by everyone, and especially by Grandma and Papa. My baby brother David who was born in my final year of high school was the star of the day. David took his first steps while visiting me to the great amusement of the whole family. He was very advanced and Mom showed much pride in him.

We went to church on the Sunday and had to recite the Rifleman's Prayer as part of the service.

> Dear God, my Father, through Thy Son
> Hear the prayer of a warrior son.
>
> Give me my eyes a vision keen
> To see the thing that must be seen.
>
> A steady hand I ask of thee
> The Feel of wind on land or sea.
>
> Let me not ever careless be
> Of life or limb or liberty.
>
> For Justice sake a quiet heart
> And grace and strength to do my part.
>
> To God and Country, Home and Corps
> Let me be faithful evermore.
>   Amen

The second week we had practice firing each day, before firing for record day on the Friday. We fired the complete marksmanship course of 100, 300 and 500 yards. How the platoon did determined what the afternoon run and PT session were to be. The DIs wanted us all to qualify on Friday. I was lucky that I had fired a rifle before. Some recruits had never used a rifle and were finding it hard to acquire the skills. We had two famous hills in Camp Mathews, named Little Agony and Big Agony. If everyone qualified we would avoid the Agonies. If our practice day score was good and most people qualified, we ran over Little Agony. If several recruits did not score well enough to qualify for at least marksman grade we ran over Big Agony several times. If the firing was very bad then the platoon had to "duck walk" (go into a full squat position and walk) up and down Big Agony. This was later stopped with newer training series platoons, after it was discovered that the full squat position tore up the knees.

Also, an individual who was not firing well had to go into the DI's tent for some "motivation." One was the "Chinese thinking position" of toes and elbows. You locked your hands behind your head and held all your weight on your toes and elbows as if you were doing a push-up (I see it in some of today's exercise programs as "the plank"). It requires a great deal of core strength to hold this position for very long. As the recruit was "thinking," the DI would lecture him on the importance of good marksmanship. The major cause of bad shooting was jerking the trigger in anticipation of the recoil of the rifle when firing. If the DI suspected this was the case, the recruit might be asked to take off his boot, the DI would have the recruit lay out his trigger finger and smash it at the finger nail with the heel of the boot, bruising it so it would hurt to jerk the trigger. This was referred to as "getting rid of the evil spirits."

When the Friday record day came, we were awarded one of three medals – the marksman, sharp shooter or expert medal depending on your final firing score – or you got nothing. If a score was not good enough then the recruit did not qualify on the rifle range and could not wear anything on his dress-uniform. Not qualifying on the range was a source of great embarrassment for a marine. The marksman's medal was what we called the "manhole cover" and was square with a target in the middle. The sharpshooter medal was a Maltese cross with the Marine Corp emblem in the middle and the expert medal was crossed rifles surrounded by a wreath.

The night before record day the DIs broke the taboo against eating pogey bait (candy) and as we were addressed as a platoon each of us was given a candy bar, the smoking lamp was lit and the DIs seemed almost human for a moment as they tried to encourage us not to be uptight and to shoot well on record day. Our platoon was in competition with the other two platoons in the training series and we needed to do better than them.

Our first day during this week started before sunrise and we were marched to the mess hall for morning chow. After eating, we had to fall in while waiting for our duty DI to take us back to the tent area. We took this opportunity to break the taboo about talking to each other and were caught by Sergeant Smallwood. This added to the day's PT as punishment. On the record day itself, as we were walking back to form the platoon, a recruit noticed Sergeant Smallwood standing behind the road about ten yards into the tree line. It was the white V of his tee-shirt in the green utility uniform that gave him away. He was standing still, which normally would allow him to go undetected. We signaled each other as we formed the platoon and stood at ease, and desisted from talking while waiting for Sergeant Smallwood, who was our duty DI, to march us back to our tent area. He duly complimented us for behaving in a military manner. We had won a small moment for ourselves over the DIs.

Only a few recruits did not qualify in Platoon 144 on record day. I had shot to expert standard on the previous two days but only qualified as a marksman on record day. I felt very disappointed. Perhaps it was the excitement of the day that caused me not to shoot as well. There was reason behind the DIs sudden change in personality the night before.

The Saturday started with the hike back to the MCRD for the next week in the training cycle.

Semper Fi: The Story of a Vietnam Era Marine

Author's mother and father with himself as a baby, Pascagoula, 1944.

a

In front of the house on Searle Avenue, 1951.
L-R: Author's grandmother, Author as a boy,
Author's grandfather ("Papa"), Sergeant Tosh.

In front of the apartment building in Montebello, Easter 1954.
L to R: Front row, Author's siblings, Sandy, Sue and Doug;
Back row, Author's father, Author,
Author's mother, Author's sister, Kitty.

Semper Fi: The Story of a Vietnam Era Marine

Mr. Empt and Author as a boy outside Mr Empt's house, 1948.

Author and siblings after a family trip to Tijuana, August 1953.
In front of the East Los Angeles house that burned down.
Front: Doug; L-R: 2nd row, Kitty and Sandy; 3rd row, Sue and Author.

Semper Fi: The Story of a Vietnam Era Marine

Platoon 144, September 1962.
Front row: L-R: Drill instructors Corporal Miller, Staff Sergeant Drake, Sergeant Yoder and Sergeant Smallwood.
Back row (*centre*): Private Orville L. Clubb.

Northern Training area, Okinawa. Swimming hole, May 1966.

Semper Fi: The Story of a Vietnam Era Marine

Boot Camp, graduation picture, 1962.

Northern Training area, Okinawa, May 1966.

Semper Fi: The Story of a Vietnam Era Marine

Operation Hastings, 15 July - 3 August 1966.
Marines of Company H, 2nd Battalion, 4th Marine Regiment,
take to the water, as they move to join up
with other elements of their battalion.
Photographer, Unknown USMC marine.

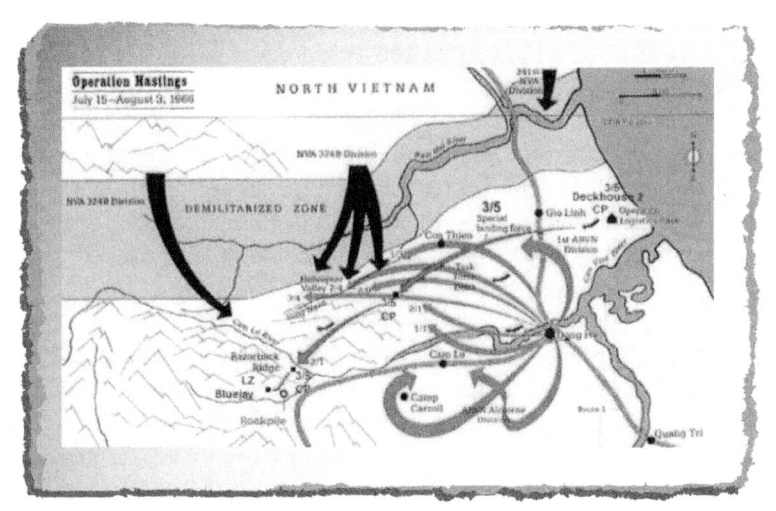

Operation Hastings sketch-map.

CHAPTER TWELVE

MCRD AFTER MARKSMANSHIP TRAINING

DURING our training cycle we had to do one week of mess duty. Mess duty was hated by all recruits and continued to be hated as we became marines. Basically, we were slaves to the full-time cooks and did the entire grunt (manual labor) work of preparing meals, washing up, scrubbing floors, cleaning tables, etc. We were servers on the chow line dishing out food to the recruits. We would wash the dishes, make the salads, etc. The day would start at 3:30 am so as to get everything ready for breakfast in time. When breakfast was done, we finished cleaning up and then preparation for lunch was begun. We again cleaned up and preparation for dinner was started. After that, we cleaned up once more and went back to the Quonset hut and waited for the next day's breakfast service. We had a break on Saturday and Sunday since only two meals were served over the weekend.

We were now more than half way through the full training cycle, which was marked by our bloused boots. We had much more close-order-drill physical fitness training ahead of us. We would go out to the grinder once a day. The grinder was an area a half-mile-long and a quarter-mile-wide, paved over with asphalt; it was like a very large parking lot without cars. Every morning at 0800 hours the garrison flag was raised. Also, the Marine Corps Recruit Depot marching band would march up and down the grinder and stop to play to the raising of the garrison flag. The drill instructors liked to get their platoons on the grinder when the band was playing. It was always a good feeling to march to the music of the band.

It was an amazing sound when everyone was in step in close-order-drill on the grinder and struck the ground with their heel at the same time. It was as if a giant animal was walking across the asphalt. For me, it became a very emotional feeling to hear the sound of the platoons, a total of over eighty recruits, moving exactly in step. It was also a source of pride for the DI to get to this form of harmony of movement. You could see the smile on his face when synchronization was achieved for the platoon and you only heard what sounded like one giant boot striking the ground. It was a time when the whole platoon was one.

We were shown how to use our bayonets and then we practiced this by means of pugil stick fighting. We were taught the Sadler system of bayonet fighting. It was modeled on boxing: the skill of boxing was translated as the use of the rifle butt and the bayonet as a fist. We assumed a stance similar to that used in boxing, holding the rifle in front of us. We visualized the bayonet as being one hand and the butt of the rifle as the other. Our basic moves were slashing, strike, parry and lunge with our rifle and bayonet. We could do something like a boxing upper cut with the butt of the rifle and we could parry or slash across the opponent's body as if delivering a punch.

After we learned the moves in practice we moved to actual pugil stick fighting. The pugil stick was a round, two-inch-thick oak pole that was as long as our rifles with their bayonets fixed. It was padded at each end and the end that represented the bayonet had a red stripe around the padding. The pugil stick could be gripped like a rifle and was approximately the same weight and length as an unloaded rifle with its bayonet.

We started by fighting members of Platoon 144 for practice and after practicing in our platoon we moved into competition bouts against the other two platoons in our training series. We were made to line up in two lines with about twenty yards in between them. When the referee (bayonet instructor) blew a whistle, the two fighting recruits would charge each other and fight until it was determined that, had a real rifle and bayonet been used, a killing blow would have been delivered. We wore a football helmet, a jock strap and boxing gloves for protection from the blows of the wooden stick.

My turn came up and I drew a big African-American man who was taller than me, wore size 15 boots and looked like a giant. My adrenalin was flowing and I was able to defeat him. I found that my reaction time was a little quicker, so I was able to parry his blow and get in a "killing blow." As a "winner" I had to line up again for another fight. As I got to the starting line again and was about to go, Sergeant Smallwood gave me my briefing and whispered, "Last time I saw this private he held his stick too high. Go in under his stick with the bayonet as you come in on him." The whistle blew and we charged each other. I followed

Sergeant Smallwood's instructions and caught my opponent square in the middle of his chest with the bayonet part of the stick, thus ending the fight with one blow, sending my opponent to the ground with the breath knocked out of him. I was now feeling very confident since I had made it through the first two rounds. I came around again and found myself facing a much smaller opponent. I figured that this fight was in the bag. The whistle blew and as I got close to my opponent he caught me up the side of the head with the butt end of the pugil stick so hard that it knocked me to the ground. The helmet provided less protection than I might have wished and I was seeing stars. I had a headache for the rest of the day.

Hand-to-hand combat was not as extensive as I was hoping for. We were told that in a fight during combat you must learn to improvise and use what you can for a weapon. As one of our platoon's black members said: "A brick, a bat and a light pair of shoes." We were taught eye gouges and various points on the enemy's body to deliver death blows. We were told that in combat there are no rules, only winners and dead people. We were shown several jujitsu-style throws and how to choke a person with a choke-out hold. Afterwards, we practiced the choke and throws on each other. We were shown the places where a killing blow could be delivered. We then practised delivering the killing blows but stopping short of a strike to the killing area.

During the second half of the training cycle we had our dress-uniforms tailored. The Marine Corps was very fussy about dress-uniforms. The pant leg had to make one fold on the front of our shoes and the back of the pant leg had to touch the top of the heel when we were standing. Our tie had to have one and only one dimple in the middle of the tied tie.

Once we had our full uniform issue, we learned how to lay out what we called "junk on the bunk," or "things on the springs." Basically, we had to lay out the whole contents of a regulation sea bag (what was called a duffle bag in the army) and our 782 gear (field equipment: packs, shovel, poncho, etc.) on our bunk bed in a predetermined order. It had to be displayed so that the name stamped on each of our garments could be seen by the inspecting officer. Normally, the inspection started with a rifle inspection, then all recruits moved to their squad bay and stood at attention by their bunks while the inspecting officer made his rounds. The officer would be looking for bad display of the issue or Irish pennants (threads or strings on the clothing).

I remember once during a rifle inspection, as we were getting closer to graduation, that I let go of the rifle so quickly the inspecting officer nearly missed it. The M14 rifle inspection starts when the inspecting officer moves in front of the recruit. The recruit lifts the rifle across his body to a position called port arms. He is holding the top part of the rifle with his left hand and the small of the rifle stock in his right. With the knife edge on the right hand, the rifle is opened and locked open (this is done by putting the knife edge on the right in contact with the operating rod and pressing the rod sharply to the rear and locking the bolt lock leaving the chamber exposed). He then lowers his head and eyes to check that the receiver (rifle chamber) does not have a round in it. He then raises his head and looks back to the front and re-grasps the small of the stock with the right hand, assuming the "inspection arms" position. When the recruit first looks ahead the inspecting officer can grab the rifle at any time. The officer normally tries to grab the rifle as fast as possible and if the recruit doesn't release the rifle as it is being grabbed, the butt of the rifle is likely to catch the recruit in the groin. When the recruit sees the movement of the inspecting officer's arm, he must release the rifle and quickly stand to attention with his arms at his side.

Platoon 144 was being inspected by our series commander, First Lieutenant Fehlen. As he was coming down the ranks I saw out of the corner of my eye that he was trying to catch the rifle before a recruit could release it. When he centered on me, I went through the drill of going to port arms, opening the bolt and looking in the chamber, and back to attention. I had had three years of practice being inspected in high school Junior Reserve Officers' Training. When I saw Lieutenant Fehlen's arm start to move I dropped my rifle and snapped my hands to my side at attention. Lieutenant Fehlen had to squat down to catch the rifle about one foot from the ground. He was shocked and stayed squatting for over a second. He stood up again but had successfully caught the rifle. He looked at me and smiled. I had to fight to hold back my smile. It was a minor contest and we had both won.

Platoon 144 graduated on Tuesday, 18 September 1962. This was a pleasant time at the MCRD when we marched up to the theater for our parents and guests to watch the graduation ceremony. It was a strange feeling getting ready to graduate. I was a little sad that it was all over; I had grown used to the routine of basic training.

My mom, brothers, sisters, Papa and Grandma came to the ceremony and to visit with me. After graduation I was allowed to lunch and spend some time with the family. My sisters had made their great potato salad and Grandma her Southern fried chicken. It was great to get some home cooking again. They had brought me several chocolate bars since we were not allowed to have pogey bait in training. I got sick after consuming two Hershey's chocolate bars. I guess that after three months with only one candy bar my body was not used to the taste.

On Friday, we boarded buses for Camp San Onofre and the Infantry Training Regiment. We were seen off by all four of our DIs. It was as if we had become family in the last few months. Now that we had graduated our DIs were treating us almost like humans and we were able to have a few chats with them as marine to marine prior to boarding the bus. I remember Corporal Miller joking with us and saying, "One day I'm going to be reporting into a new unit and have to salute one of you dumb fucks. I'm sure that some of you will some day be officers." Even Sergeant Yoder almost seemed as if he could be human. He was telling us how group behavior is predictable; whereas the actions of individuals are very hard to predict. The DIs take advantage of this group predictability. He told us that if punishment was given to the whole platoon because of one individual's behavior, the platoon would in turn punish that individual.

CHAPTER THIRTEEN

INFANTRY TRAINING REGIMENT

IN 1962, all marines had to go through four weeks with the Infantry Training Regiment no matter what their military occupation specialty was to be. We were told we were rifleman first and our MOS was second. It was a very intense twenty-eight days of being on the move all the time.

When we arrived at Camp San Onofre we were met by the equivalent of a receiving drill instructor at the Marine Corps Recruit Depot, a non-commissioned officer. Instead of wearing the "Smokey Bear hat" of a DI he was wearing a helmet liner painted green. As we got off the bus we fell into platoon formation and the receiving NCO of the training regiment did a roll call. As he called each of our names we would answer "yo" or "here." We were proud now that we were being called "Marine," instead of the hundreds of belittling names the DIs could create, and thought that we were now over the "sir, yes sir" phase. But to our surprise, the receiving ITR NCO scolded us for not making sure that "sir" was the first and last word out of our mouth. We were told that during ITR we would continue to use "sir" as the first and last word when speaking to anyone who was a fully vested marine. We were going to have to finish ITR to earn the right to drop the "sir" when speaking to anyone senior. We thought that this necessity would be over now that we had graduated from basic training. However, it was still an improvement because we were at least hailed or referred to as "Marine." Our time in the ITR was strict but not as demanding as basic training.

For some marines, it was a big disappointment to learn that they would have to do mess duty or guard duty before getting into a training company. I was lucky in that I was scheduled to go back to the MCRD to attend electronics school and needed to get through my infantry training and take my after training leave quickly. I was assigned to C Company and started ITR training on the 24 September 1962. C Company was made up of those of us who needed to get to specialist schools from the MCRD training series. It was sad to part with some of my Platoon 144 training mates who had to do mess or guard duty.

The ITR training was four weeks of constant activity. About every aspect of infantry training was packed into the time allowed. We were issued with M1 rifles for this phase of instruction. For many ITR marines this was their first encounter with the M1. Since I had handled an M1 in the Junior Reserve Officers' Training Corps at high school I was familiar with the rifle but had never fired it. At Garfield High we had a .22 rifle range and were allowed to fire the .22s but we never fired our issued M1. In fact, if I remember correctly, our JROTC M1s may even have had the firing pin removed. However, I already knew how the M1 functioned and how to break down the rifle and clean it.

For me, one of the more memorable parts of ITR was live fire training. We learned as a squad how to attack a machine gun or other fortified position by flanking it. This was done with live fire, where two fire teams would lay down fire from the front, while the attacking fire team would get the position on the flank. It had to be executed correctly since we were using live fire, and the front firing two fire teams had to stop firing as the flanking fire team overran the position. There are thirteen marines in a squad divided into three fire teams of four marines each, with one squad leader.

Also, for live fire training we had to crawl along a live fire course covered with barbed wire, with a machine gun firing live ammo above us and explosives going off all around us.

One evening, we saw the fire power of a "platoon on line." We sat in bleachers (tiered rows of seats) behind a platoon that was set up as if on a perimeter and were to fire with all tracer rounds. That way we could see the overlapping fields of fire. The demo started and it looked like a solid wall of bullets. The riflemen were firing in their fields of fire marked with a stick on either side of the front of the hole. The machine guns were raking across the riflemen's fields of fire. It looked like nothing could live through such fire power. Then we reversed positions and we did the live fire while the other group observed from the bleachers. Live fire has a way of waking up your senses.

Most evenings were filled. We went out and stayed out a lot of the evenings in our twenty-eight days. I remember we were sent off on a compass course as fire teams and needed to find our way back to a designated point using just a map and compass.

This took up the larger part of one night and we slept in the field. I also remember that after one night in the field I woke up in the morning to find a big tarantula sitting on top of my sleeping bag on my chest. I got up very slowly so that it fell to the ground. There was scuttlebutt (rumor) that a few months earlier a marine in ITR woke up with a rattlesnake in his sleeping bag. It was looking for warmth as was the tarantula on my chest.

We had a class in camouflage. We were made to sit in bleachers overlooking an open field and were told that there were two marines in this field watching us. Then we were asked if we could find them while we remained seated and were given ten minutes to do this. We were allowed to talk to each other and work as a group. Time ran out and we could not spot them. The two marines were then told to stand up. To our surprise they were very close to us. As the class continued, it was explained how we could camouflage ourselves. We learned that any straight line was normally man-made and that nature rarely came in straight lines. My mind popped back to Sergeant Smallwood and how the white of his tee-shirt in his green utilities had made a straight, white V that gave him away.

Probably the most memorable training exercise was the gas chamber. The gas used in the chamber was chlorobenzylidene malonitrile, or CS gas, also known as tear gas. Each marine in ITR spent approximately three to five minutes in the gas chamber; this was probably one of the longest three to five minutes of our lives.

Before the exercise we were briefed on how we were to enter the gas chamber. We were told to go in holding the right shoulder of the marine in front with our right hand and with our masks donned and clear, but once the doors were sealed, the masks were to come off. When inside the chamber we were to form a circle around the wall with the instructors in the middle. The first exercise was to break the seal of our mask, which would allow us to breathe in a little of the gas, but just as the eyes began to stream and the coughing set in, we would put our mask back on and clear it. The next step was to remove the mask and hold it in front of us. On instruction, we were to sing the Marine Corps hymn and run around the chamber clockwise in a circle till the instructor told us to stop and don the gas mask and clear it again. We would then file out of the gas chamber the same way that we had come in with each marine putting his right hand on the right shoulder of the marine in front.

After the briefing, we were brought to a tent similar to the ones at Camp Matthews. It had a permanent floor and a tear gas canister had been set off inside. We were divided into small groups of about ten to twelve marines and entered the tent in these groups as the inside of the gas chamber was small. Again, we were briefed that once inside the tent the instructor was going to tell us when to remove the mask, etc. It all seemed clear and I was in the first group.

As my group got inside and the door was closed, one marine started to panic because his gas mask was not sealed properly and was leaking. He ran for the door and tried to open it. This caused a panic among the rest of the group and sent some other marines rushing to the door. Soon the majority of the ITR marines in the gas chamber were trying to get through the closed door. It was totally blocked with panicking marines. It was a stampede with nowhere to go. One of the instructors on the outside heard the commotion and opened the door. He started to grab and pull out any marines who were trapped. When I was pulled out I fell to the ground coughing, with my eyes burning very badly and my nose running. My exposed skin was burning in a way similar to having sunburn. Everyone was coughing and a couple of marines vomited. I now understood why people do not like to be gassed with tear gas by the police. Of course the next groups of marines went through the exercise flawlessly. After all the other groups had been in we were allowed to go in one more time and do the exercise correctly, which we did. We spent more than twice as much time in the gas chamber as everyone else that day because of the panic. The objective of the exercise was to help the marines control their fear and to develop a belief in the ability of their gas mask to protect them if they were gassed.

The flame thrower made another lasting impression on me. It was made up of two tanks carried on your back with a hose and firing device to direct the flame. You would hold the flame-throwing device of the weapon with both hands in a similar way to holding a rifle. The front of the nozzle had a "match" to light the flame. The back of the nozzle had a trigger to fire the napalm. To fire, you would strike the match by squeezing the two sides of the match together in your left hand and pull the trigger, pointing at the intended target. The blast of heat that came back made you realize that the receiving end of this weapon must be terrifying.

We were also taken to a range that was used for explosives training and taught how to set off C4 explosives by putting a blasting cap in a block of C4 explosive material. The instructor demonstrated how to take a length of fuse and put an ignition device on one side and a blasting cap on the other. The length of the fuse determined the time to the explosion. The blasting cap had to be crimped with a crimping tool that looked like a pair of pliers. He demonstrated crimping by holding the blasting cap behind himself low down and then crimping the blasting cap onto the fuse. We were told that this was done in case the blasting cap exploded. If it exploded behind your posterior it was better than having it explode in front of you. He went on to say: "A human ass has the most tissue and an explosion here will cause less damage to someone preparing an explosive; if it goes off in front of you, you can lose your balls." This sounded like good advice.

Each of us was then given a half-pound block of C4, a fuse and an ignition device; we had to put the explosive together by putting on the ignition device and crimping the blasting cap. We then walked out to the range where there were several large holes; we each inserted our explosive into an open hole and on command we ignited it by pulling the ignition device. We then shouted: "FIRE IN THE HOLE." When given permission we were to walk back to the safety area. We were told never to run! Of course, when we first shouted "fire in the hole" the instructor said that he couldn't hear us. We were standing over our holes watching the fuse of the explosive burn down to the blasting cap. After about the third or fourth shout we were allowed to walk back to the safety area to watch our explosives go off.

During ITR we were also taken to a 3.5 rocket launcher range. The 3.5 was the replacement for the bazooka of WWII. It fired a bigger rocket and could be broken into two nearly equal-sized pieces for easy transportation. The range had several old shot-out tanks across a ravine about 200 yards away. We were given instruction on how to work in a team of two to fire the weapon, with one man as the loader and the other as shooter. The shooter would place the weapon on his right shoulder and sight in on the target. The loader would insert the rocket and pull a lever to arm the launcher. He would then tap the shooter on the helmet twice and face aft holding his fingers in his ears. When the rocket launched it produced a terrible back-blast. I was loader first and my team shooter did not hit the target tank. As the shooter, I noticed that the rocket moved the launching tube up as the rocket travelled down the tube, making a very accurate shot hard for a person not familiar with the weapon. I also missed the tank.

My favorite weapon was the Browning automatic rifle (BAR). The M14 was to replace the BAR and the M1, but it was too light to be as accurate as the BAR. The BAR had a nice feel to it when you fired it. However, it weighed nineteen pounds and was harder to carry for long distances. I remember an exercise where we had to jump from hole to hole and fire a different weapon from each, one of which was a BAR. The BAR part of the range had a target that was a pill box about 200 yards away. The objective was to fire bursts of rounds and get as many rounds as possible through the front square hole of the pill box. I don't remember the other weapons but the BAR hole came around several times and I was able to get rounds through the hole of the pill box after only one burst. On the third time around the course the instructor at the BAR station of the range said, "Marine, you're deadly with the BAR." This gave me a great sense of pride.

After our twenty-eight days of training we were given leave. By now most of the members of C Company had colds and some had upper respiratory infections from lack of sleep and getting chilled in the field. However, none of us wanted to go to sick bay because we wanted to go home. So I took my cold home for thirty days of recovery on the 21 October 1962.

CHAPTER FOURTEEN

HOME LEAVE AND THE MISSILES OF OCTOBER 1962

I went home to La Puente, California, during my home leave, but tried to spend most of my time with my classmates from Garfield High. However, there was a general feeling everywhere that the world was about to go up in flames. In September, while I was in the Infantry Training Regiment, Soviet-made medium-range nuclear missiles were discovered on the island of Cuba. On 22 October 1962, President Kennedy addressed the American people about the buildup of arms on Cuba, just in time for my home leave. He announced that US warships would immediately stop all Soviet vessels bound for Cuban shores. For the next several days the world hovered on the brink of a nuclear war. We now know that feverish negotiations were going on between Kennedy and Khrushchev to end the crisis. The crisis played out through the month of October and gave my home leave a different feeling from what I had been expecting. This was the most serious foreign policy crisis of the Kennedy term in the Oval Office. It may have been the most serious foreign policy crisis in the history of the Cold War. Cuba is only ninety miles from the coast of Florida, and missiles fired from Cuba could easily strike cities in the United States as far north as Cincinnati, and as far west as San Antonio – and with minimal warning time. Also, Kennedy felt that American prestige (as well as his own) was on the line.

In high school, I had developed a crush on a young woman named Zulema. She was originally from Corpus Christi, Texas, and was very sophisticated in my eyes. She was working and I was trying every way possible to spend time with her. I met her after work and we talked about the crisis that was playing out. She told me about her parents storing away canned goods and other essential items just in case. I talked about the fact that as a newly recruited marine I was not sure what would happen to me. I was hoping that I would be able to go to electronics school as per my orders. No one was sure of the future.

I tried to make the home leave as normal as possible and went to church with Zulema over on the other side of town in West

Los Angeles on the Sunday after I arrived home, wearing my dress blues trying to impress her. As we left the church, the priest was waiting on the front steps greeting people who were leaving and shook my hand. It was a great feeling to be with Zulema for the church service. Also, I took her to see the movie *The Longest Day*, again wearing my dress blues. Whenever I got a letter from her while in basic and infantry training I would treasure it.

However, I found out that she had a boyfriend who was the choir leader at the church that we had attended and she was crazy about him. I remember going over to her house and she was listening to Handel's *Messiah*, which was his favorite piece of music (and of course hers). Since she was so crazy about this man I figured I did not have a chance and finally went through a period of heartbreak and forgot her.

Those of my friends who were already working did not have much time for me, so I would go to Garfield and hang out in my uniform trying to impress the friends that had not yet graduated from high school.

On leave, I met up again with a girl named Connie whom I had always admired and who had been two years below me at Garfield. She had just broken up with her boyfriend who was in the marching band with her. She agreed to write to me. It helped me with the heartbreak over Zulema. I had not done well on the dating scene at Garfield as I did not have a car. I really liked Connie; she was different from Zulema and very attractive in other ways. She was a very nice young woman. She'd had a very traditional Mexican upbringing and I thought she'd make an excellent family person.

Grandma and Papa had sold the house on Searle Avenue while I was in high school and had bought a three-bedroom house in Pomona to be closer to Mom and the grandchildren in California. I stayed with them for a couple of days of my leave and enjoyed it.

Perhaps ignorance is bliss! Staying with Papa and Grandma I learned that Papa was now having trouble with his beliefs. He had found out that the two major Christian holy days of Christmas and Easter were pagan in origin. Both these holy days had been adopted into Christianity by the Romans to make it easy to convert the masses to Christianity.

He had found out that, although the Bible story speaks of Jesus being born at a time when shepherds were tending their fields at night, most scholars think that it would have been far too cold in December for shepherds to be in the fields. He had also discovered that Christmas was really the celebration of the winter solstice. – Julius Caesar, in 46 BCE, in establishing his Julian calendar had determined December 25 as the date of the winter solstice in Europe. – There was a pagan festival associated with the solstice and Papa learned that the Roman Church had adopted the winter solstice festival as Christmas. He had spent many hours studying books on religion trying to find the truth.

He was equally horrified when he found out that Easter was also a holy day adopted from another religion. He learned that Easter is linked to the Jewish Passover by much of its symbolism, as well as by its position in the calendar. In most European languages, the feast called Easter in English is known by the words for Passover in those languages; and in the older English versions of the Bible the word Easter is used to translate Passover. Relatively newer elements such as the Easter Bunny and Easter egg hunts have become part of the holiday's celebrations, participated in by many Christians and non-Christians alike. – The rabbit and egg symbolize fertility and the arrival of spring. – Some Christian denominations do not celebrate Easter. Papa told me that he now realised that Easter was basically a celebration of spring.

During my leave, to help him in his research, I bought Papa a book of the works of Flavius Josephus, a Jewish historian who wrote at around the time of Jesus. Papa tried to get more information on the two holy days at a Bible study class at Sister Lee's church and was thrown out of the church as a result. Papa continued with his quest to find the truth and it was having a big effect on him.

I remember also that Papa had taken up running and was doing five miles a day. I went with him for a jog. It was a good go for a man well into his late sixties or early seventies. He was happy and very healthy. However, after I went back to active duty I learned that his doctor advised him to quit running since it was "unhealthy" for him.

My family came to have a Sunday dinner (lunch in Southern talk) at Papa and Grandma's house in Pomona while I was there. As we settled into the meal, I was very relaxed and committed a great violation of verbal usage when I asked Dad to "pass the fucking mashed potatoes!" The word "fuck" had been used so many times in training that it had become part of our vernacular. I think that everyone at the table heard it but chose to ignore it. I realized what I had said the moment I had finished the sentence. Thereafter, I had to really be on my guard when speaking.

While I was on leave, Dad still did not give me much respect, even though I was only visiting and now out of the house and earning my own money. He would still verbally abuse me. I now used the tactic of just ignoring him. The twenty-eight days of leave went by very quickly and it was time to go back to the Marine Corp Recruit Depot for school. It had been a hard leave trying to deal with my cold and my dad.

I was glad to report back to active duty.

CHAPTER FIFTEEN

ELECTRONICS SCHOOL MCRD

I arrived at the Marine Corp Recruit Depot after my home leave in the third week of November 1962 to attend electronics school. We were housed in the barracks that made up the side of the grinder close to the garrison flag and we were in class sizes of around twenty students. There was one week of classes for each subject with a test on the Friday. We would get up at 0500 hours and be in class by 0700 hours. We would have noon chow and finish in the afternoon around 1600 hours, giving us eight hours of class each day. After class we would have PT, then shower, have evening chow and then would normally study till lights out at 2130 hours.

We were allowed liberty (leave from the base) each evening and on weekends. However, if we failed a test and got put back or if our score at the end of a subject examination was low, there would be no liberty and we had to attend an evening study hall. We were told that if we failed an end-of-subject test once, we would be put back a week but if we failed twice in any subject or failed once in two different subjects we would be sent to the infantry as a 0311 rifleman. – In those days, the Marine Corp comprised the air wing (the Wing) and the infantry. Together they were known as the Fleet Marine Force (FMF). We used to joke and call the FMF the "Fighting Mother Fuckers." – Everyone wanted to get into the Wing since the duty was much nicer.

The first week's subject was mathematics and the instructor started on Monday morning with the formula 2+2=4. By Friday, we were well into trigonometry since we needed to understand the mathematics of sine wave behavior. If a student fell asleep the instructor would throw the chalk or blackboard eraser at the sleeping student trying to hit him in the face. They must have had a lot of practice since they were very accurate and normally hit the student's face and startled him.

I found this first week hard-going as I only had high school algebra and did not have the study habits needed to handle the amount of homework and material given. I was getting bad headaches from reading. Friday came and I barely passed the end-of-subject examination. I was sent to sickbay for my headaches, where it was found that I was far-sighted and I was issued reading glasses.

I was lucky in some ways; several of the young marines in the school had discovered Tijuana while on liberty and had failed the first week's test. The ones that failed were set back one week, and if they failed the second time or another class, they were sent for basic infantry training (BIT) at the school at Camp Pendleton, to complete their training as a 0311 (infantry rifleman) military occupation specialty.

At the start of electronics school I made several friends who would remain friends for the time of my active duty. One was Jimmy Dean Clay, who was to become my brother-in-law, and another was a wild man named Gordy. We always called each other by our last names or nicknames. Clay was older; he was already over twenty-one and a great friend as he was mature. I could always go to him for advice and really enjoyed his company. Gordy had been put in the brig (jail) during basic training as a recruit for sneaking out and exploring the MCRD. Gordy had waited till lights out, bloused his boots, opened his top button and wandered around the depot. The duty DI caught him and he was sent to the brig for his offence. He did not seem to have any fear and was considered a mad man. One time, Gordy went to the San Diego Zoo and stole a small, live alligator from the alligator enclosure. He brought it back in his laundry bag, flooded the barracks' shower area and let the alligator go. Inevitably it scared several people coming in for a shower. He thought this was great fun.

In the second week, I was put on study hall and not allowed evening liberty. The second week's classes were basic electronics. Again, I did badly at the end-of-week subject test. I was called in for interview about my grades and warned that if I did badly in the next end-of-subject test I would be sent to the telephone and teletype repair classes instead of radio or radar repair. The system was that if we passed all our courses with good grades we were streamed into the full electronics school for radio, radio relay or radar repair. Otherwise, we were put into the telephone and teletype repair stream. Streaming for telephone and teletype repair was done after our fourth week of class.

The third week was basic electronics and I did reasonably well and was taken off the study hall. However, after the first streaming I found myself in the telephone and teletype repair group instead of continuing on in electronics. I guess my performance in the third and fourth weeks was not enough to change the decision of the school.

While at the telephone and teletype repair school, a regulation was discovered which had been forgotten, that a US Marine officer had to be able to do a fifty-mile forced march in full combat gear in less than twenty-four hours. There was a lot of publicity about this fitness test and officers throughout the Corps took the test. How they did we never learned.

Three of us studying in the school decided to take the challenge as well even though we were enlisted men and the regulations did not apply to ourselves. We had it set up so that we could get started early and were able to have morning chow before the mess hall formally opened for the others in the school. After morning chow, we donned our full combat gear and started on the pre-measured course. We had to do twenty-five laps around a two-mile course. We were planning on running one lap then walking a lap.

We started the test at 0400 hours on a Saturday. We were jogging for the first lap and finished it in less than half an hour. We decided to continue to run and we were still running at five thirty in the morning when reveille was sounded for the recruits. By now we had covered over four of the twenty-five laps. I smelled the toothpaste of the recruits brushing their teeth and it made me nauseated. I fell back and vomited up my morning chow and told my other two friends to continue; I would catch up.

I realized that the previous eight and more miles in full combat gear were taking their toll. I started a system of running and walking, trying to keep the other two in sight. It worked for a while but after another hour they were finally out of sight as they had not stopped to walk the alternate laps.

I continued walking and running and trying to catch sight of the other two, who must have been at least a mile ahead of me. Little did I know that they had slowed down and had also begun to walk the laps. At about 10:00 am, I rounded the corner of the course that gave on to a one-mile straight stretch and saw that I was catching up on them. By now, I was so tired that I started only to walk but when it seemed that I was not closing the space I started walking and running again.

A little after noon, I finally caught up with them. The running had taken its toll on them also and we all decided that we were going to have to walk the last part of the course if we were going to finish. We surely did want to finish since it would have been a great loss of face to quit. The effort was highly publicized and a lot of special arrangements had been made for us to attempt the fitness test.

We continued walking and finally finished the course in less than eleven hours at around 3:00 pm. As we approached the finish line, we all locked arms and crossed the line together. It was not exactly what we had set out to achieve but we had finished the test in less than half the allotted time. We were allowed back in the mess hall to get something to eat even though it was Saturday and normally only two meals were served.

I went back to the squad bay and had a shower. I lay down on my rack and fell asleep. I was finally woken up by a friend who wanted to go to the evening movie on base at the MCRD's theater. As I got up I realized that my legs were so sore that I could hardly stand. I walked to the movie but it was an effort. I had never gotten sore from exercise so quickly before. I was sore for a few days.

I went through the training for telephone and teletype repair and was mostly third out of a class of eighteen. I dropped back towards the end of the course and graduated fifth out of eighteen students.

CHAPTER SIXTEEN

POSTING TO 1ST MARINE DIVISION

MY first posting after telephone and teletype repair school was with the Communications Company of the Headquarters Battalion of the 1st Marine Division, sometime around March 1963. I was there as part of a group of technicians who kept the electrical and electronic communications equipment running for Division Headquarters. We had radio technicians, radio relay technicians, and telephone and teletype technicians, etc. It seemed to me that it was a better duty than being in an infantry battalion. I quickly settled into a routine of working in the shop.

I had totally given up on Zulema and I was now writing serious letters to Connie in Los Angeles and had become infatuated with her. Connie's family was a traditional Mexican family and insisted that I could not go anywhere with Connie unless chaperoned by her younger sister. We would see each other very little. Even though I was not physically able to see her, it was great getting mail from her. Receiving mail was a precious thing. We were having a snail-mail relationship similar to today's virtual relationships over the internet. To me, mail had become a lifeline. If I got a letter from Connie I would always turn first to the salutation to see if it was signed with "love" to assure myself that I still had a girlfriend.

The Marines had been integrated for a while but there was still a lot of racial tension between blacks and whites. The sixties were turbulent times for race relations and the Corps had its share of incidents. When I joined the 1st Marine Division Headquarters it was the first time that I came across the terms "splibs" and "chucks." I was told by an African-American marine that the terms had their origins in Swahili and that "splib" meant a superior man. Blacks were splibs and whites were chucks. The African-American marines were very proud to be called splib, as it was seen as "hip," but I'm not so sure that chuck was such a compliment if the term had its origins in Swahili.

I normally went home every other weekend to my parents' home in La Puente if I wasn't on duty. After we'd started in electronics school, Clay had begun to go home with me. He continued to do this after we were both posted to the Communications Company. As he was already twenty-one, he could buy alcohol. If we did not go home together, then Clay and I would go to Tijuana or go skin diving together. He was a great friend.

Clay once saved my life while we were skin diving off La Jolla. On this particular weekend we snorkeled at a small beach that was surrounded by rocks and had two very big rock formations a little way out to sea. Clay and I snorkeled out between these two rock formations and after a while we became very cold. The low water temperature in the Pacific off California will reduce your body temperature very fast. We started to swim back to shore between the two rock formations but I developed leg cramps. I had a brand new spear gun and was not about to lose it. I was swimming with only one arm. By then Clay had already made it to shore. I remembered earlier seeing seals basking on the rocks so I made an attempt to climb over the rocks to the calmer water on the other side. As I was climbing up, a large wave broke over me slamming me into the rock and washing me to the other side into the calm waters. I remember sinking to the bottom and looking up at the surface and thinking how calm and peaceful I felt. I knew I was dead. Then I felt arms grab me under my armpits and pull me to the surface. It was Clay; he had seen what had happened and come back in to assist me. As I got on shore I saw that I had been cut up very badly by the rocks. I had a very deep gash on my right hand that was bleeding profusely. This was Saturday and I wrapped a towel around my injured hand and put pressure on the wound to stop the bleeding. I did not go to the sickbay till Monday. When the corpsman saw the wound on Monday he scolded me for not coming in immediately and getting it stitched. I later learned that if I had gone to the side of one of the rock formations rather than going through the middle the current would have brought me to shore.

We had a divisional exercise where we were picked up on a beach at Camp Pendleton with landing craft and taken to a ship offshore. We were then made to climb up the cargo nets to board the ship. Once on board we were there for a day and then had to go ashore again, climbing back down the cargo nets to the landing craft. Going down we used the rule "feet on the horizontals and hands on the verticals." This referred to the configuration of the cargo net as it hung over the side of the ship; we grabbed the vertical rope with our hands and put our feet on the horizontal ropes. When I got to the bottom of the cargo net I realized that getting off the net required timing. There was a five-foot swell and the deck of the landing craft would first be by my foot then it would drop five feet down. There is an art in leaving a cargo net to board a landing craft. You have to time your step off the cargo net to coincide with the rising of the landing craft. Once we were all back aboard the landing craft we headed for the beach, and as soon as the front ramp of the landing craft dropped we had to disembark quickly. We were instructed to run off the side of the ramp rather than the middle since the landing craft was working back and forth and you could break a leg if the ramp were to catch you.

Division Headquarters was not a bad duty but when I went home on the weekends I was getting a lot of pressure from Mom to try for a hardship discharge and come home. She said that she needed me to help with the family since Dad was so unreliable. I figured that I did not have a very good case since both Mom and Dad were working. But she still had a lot of influence over my actions and decisions, and she convinced me to apply for a hardship discharge. I don't know what I was thinking as I did not get along with Dad at all. As I anticipated would happen, I was refused the hardship discharge. Mom got very upset and I began to feel guilty that I had not stayed at home after high school and helped her out. However, Dad was making my life miserable and it had been a good choice to leave by joining the Corps. Anyway, if I had not joined the Marines I would have been drafted into the US Army. As the application was denied, I had no choice but to continue my enlistment.

I was soon after this given a week's guard duty, which everyone must do from time to time. I had to move to the guard barracks for the week and would walk a post for four hours every night. It was very tiring and I remember that one night while walking the post in the motor pool (the army vehicle parking lot) I became very sleepy. I saw a light about fifty yards away and after blinking my eyes I found myself standing under the light. I had walked the full fifty yards asleep and had no memory of doing so.

On one of the days of guard duty, I was given a work detail to supervise four prisoners who were to cut grass and clean the lawn in front of the Division Headquarters building. I had four rounds of ammunition in the magazine of my M14 and did not wish to allow them to escape. There was one round for each prisoner. We believed that if we allowed a prisoner to escape we had to serve his time. I'm not sure if that was true but it was certainly a motivator to make sure we kept the prisoners from running.

On another day, I was appointed as a brig chaser (marine assigned to escort prisoners). I had to wear my class B dress-uniform (dress khaki summer uniform) and get a prisoner from the brig and take him to his court martial. At the guard armory I was issued a .45 with a full magazine and given a jeep and a driver. I was driven to the brig. When I arrived at the brig I had to remove my .45, take out the magazine and check in the pistol and magazine at a desk between the first and second gate of the brig. Then I was allowed entry through the second gate to pick up the prisoner.

There were lines painted throughout the brig and the prisoners would have to request permission to cross each line. The prisoner was marched out by a prison guard and taken to get his papers to take to the court martial. There was a window where he was to pick up the papers, which was where I waited. The prisoner was stood behind a red line by the prison guard and then had to shout, "Sir, permission to cross the red line, sir." The guard at the window gave him permission to approach the window. He approached the window and received the paperwork. The inside chaser turned the prisoner over to me and I marched him out through the inside gate. I stopped him while I picked up my .45, inserted the rounds into the magazine, put the gun back in my holster, and then marched him through the outside gate to the jeep.

As we settled in the back of the jeep, he looked at me smiling and asked, "What are you going to do if I run?" In my best Clint Eastwood voice I replied, "I'm going to shoot your fucking ass." The driver said, "I think he is going to get six, six and a kick" (six months in the brig, loss of six month's pay and a Bad Conduct or Dishonorable Discharge). "I've seen this shitbird before! He thinks he's a real bad ass; if you shoot him you'll do the Corps a favor and we will not have to waste so much fucking time on him." Nothing else was said throughout the rest of the journey.

I marched the prisoner into the courtroom and had to wait outside till the first day of the trial was over, which was all day! It was a very boring day just sitting and waiting. Then I had to go through the same procedure in reverse to get him back to the brig.

The week of guard duty soon ended and I went back to my unit and the normal daily routines in the Communications Company.

One afternoon while thinking about my family life and the unsuccessful application for a hardship discharge, I decided that I would end it all and commit suicide. I bought myself a large bottle of aspirin tablets from the Post Exchange (PX). Reason, however, took over and I just put the bottle in my foot locker. Since the rejection of my hardship discharge I had been experiencing bouts of depression. Now that I had the aspirins, I continued to experience the depression but would normally decide that suicide was not a good option and put the aspirins away again.

One day the depression was really unbearable and I took out the bottle of aspirin tablets and swallowed the whole lot. I went into the recreation room where I saw a couple of my fellow technicians and sat down very bleary eyed. One of them saw that I was looking strange and asked, "What the fuck is wrong with you?" I looked and him, smiled and said, "I'm committing suicide; I just swallowed a big bottle of aspirins." He replied, "Are you shitting me?" I looked back, smiled again and said, "I'm not shitting you." Just then another marine walked into the rec room and the marine who had asked me what was wrong, laughed and said to the newly arrived marine, "Clubb says he is committing suicide. Look at him." He looked at me and asked, "What are doing?" I replied, "I just took a big bottle of aspirins." He looked back at the marine who was laughing and said, "You dumb fuck, we need to get him to sickbay!" They took both my arms and started to walk me. I did not resist.

I was taken to the company office and was sent to the hospital in a company Mighty Mite Jeep. On arrival, I was put on a table and a long rubber tube with a funnel on the end was put down my throat into my stomach. It was uncomfortable and I was gagging. I had trouble breathing with the tube down my throat. Water or some solution was poured into the funnel and the tube pulled out. I vomited immediately into a pan by the bedside. The vomit was examined to see how many aspirins came up. The sickbay corpsmen asked me the size of the bottle of aspirins and I told them it was the biggest I could get from the PX. They told me that it probably was not enough to kill me but it was best to clear out my stomach. I was kept in the hospital overnight for observation. One of the corpsmen told me that I was not really trying to commit suicide but crying for help.

The next day I went back to my unit and by now the word had got around about what had happened. It seemed as if I had a contagious disease as my fellow marines avoided me. I was sent to see a naval psychiatrist two days later. I had an hour's appointment and was able to open up about my family and the trouble at home and how I wanted to return home to help.

After a week or so back at my unit people were slowly accepting me again, seeing me as just a troubled young man and not dangerous. My friend Gordy told me that some day he would commit suicide, but would do it with a bullet to the head. He said that taking pills was too easy.

I was going to the psychiatrist weekly. On my second appointment I asked the psychiatrist about the possibility of getting a hardship discharge. He looked at me and said, "I'm not going to let you go back into that mess; you're in the Corps and you're going to see it through! You're not getting out, so you need to accept that you will finish your enlistment!" That was a turning point for me.

After a month I saw the psychiatrist every other week until after a further two months he told me there was no need to return. I was sad since I enjoyed having a person with whom I could be open and not have to worry about my innermost secrets being spread around. I was feeling better and the attempted suicide made me realize that I did not want to try that again.

On the morning of 23 November 1963, we were having both a rifle and a" junk on the bunk" inspection. We had just finished the rifle inspection and were about to start the "junk on the bunk" when someone from the company office came over and told us that President Kennedy had been shot. A marine took out his radio from his wall locker and we all gathered around the radio in the barracks to hear what was happening. No one could believe that it was true. I looked over and saw that one of the marines had tears flowing down his cheeks. It was as if we were all in shock. We learned that President Kennedy was shot at around 12:30 and that at 13:00 Central Standard Time (CST), which was 19:00 Zulu time (Greenwich Mean Time), after a priest had administered the sacrament of Extreme Unction, the president was pronounced dead. It was thought that the president was already dead by the time he had arrived at the hospital. The inspection was called off immediately and we were given liberty from noon for the weekend since it was a Friday. Normally it is a joyful occasion to get extra liberty; however, I could not enjoy the weekend as our Commander in Chief had been assassinated. The whole world was in shock that weekend.

December came and went without much happening. I had had Christmas at home with the family and was now realizing that the psychiatrist was right; I did not want to get back into the mess at home. My family was completely dysfunctional and made the family from the much later television series, *The Simpsons*, look like they were normal. Dad was an alcoholic and Mom was always nagging. It would at times come to physical blows. It was as if they fed off each other and that they enjoyed it. I had a great advantage over my brothers and sisters in that I had had a few years of a stable loving family life while living with my grandparents.

On 1 January 1964, I was given mess duty. Mess duty was for a whole month. As in basic training, we got up at 3:45 am to start the day and finished at about 8:00 pm having cleaned up after the evening meal. It was boring work, constantly preparing for meals and cleaning up.

Later on in January, one of the marines on mess duty came over to me on a break and said, "Listen to this!" – The Beatles song, "I Want to Hold Your Hand", was playing. He was telling me the group was going to be famous and how great this song was. I was not as sure as he was and had never heard of the Beatles.

In the last week of mess duty I got a letter from Connie saying that she didn't want to see me or write to me anymore. This was a great blow and I felt as if I wanted to die, but I knew that I did not wish to commit suicide. I was heartbroken and could not eat. I would lie awake at night and wanted to cry. I was devastated. I wrote several letters asking her to reconsider what she had said but got no reply. Like most wounds, time is the best medicine; but at the time the pain was overwhelming.

But back to my normal routine. I was called into the company office one day and asked if I wished to transfer to a sub unit of the Division. It was in the 3/5 (3rd Battalion 5th Marine Regiment) area of Camp Margarita and it dealt with the rotation of battalions between Pendleton and Okinawa. I said I did not think that I was interested. I soon found out it was not a voluntary transfer and that I had orders to report to Sub Unit # 1.

CHAPTER SEVENTEEN

SUB UNIT #1, 1ST MARINE DIVISION

I reported to Sub Unit # 1 stationed at Camp Margarita, in the 3/5 area. The job of Sub Unit # 1 was to act as a caretaker for a battalion area and the equipment till a rotation between Camp Pendleton and Okinawa could take place. The Camp Pendleton battalion would be transported by ship to Okinawa with only their personal gear. When they arrived in Okinawa, the personnel from the battalion in Okinawa would start the trip back to Camp Pendleton. This created a space of a couple of months when no battalion was at Camp Pendleton as the journeys in both directions were being made by sea. This arrangement made a lot of sense because the equipment needed by the battalion did not have to move with the battalion. You simply changed personnel and changed the battalion identity depending on location: Okinawa (3rd Marine Division) or Camp Pendleton (1st Marine Division).

Sub Unit # 1 was a skeleton Headquarters and Service (H&S) Company, it had S6 (communication) personnel consisting of one of each type of technician (radio, radio-relay, radar, and telephone and teletype). We had S4 (supply) personnel to look after the supply area and a complete S1 (administration) clerical office. Also, we took care of those who did not rotate with their battalion. Those left behind were marines who were not able to rotate because of medical reasons, did not have enough time left on their enlistment to make the rotation, or were being discharged for any number of reasons. For example, we had some marines who were or claimed to be gay and were given an Undesirable Discharge. Others had been to the brig and were being mustered out as undesirables.

As I arrived at the 3/5 Battalion office with my sea bag, I was told by the clerk to wait as I had to report to the HNIC. I was puzzled. The clerk said, "The head nigger in charge," and he laughed. One must remember this was the 1960s. I found out that Sub Unit # 1 was made up purely of enlisted men; we did not have any officers. Our head non-commissioned officer was Master Sergeant Erastus Johnson, Jr. I reported in and found him to be a pleasant man. Johnson was a big African-American and extremely muscular. He was a veteran of the Korean War and it was said that he had been with the Military Police in Saigon before Sub Unit #1. I learned that everyone really loved the old man. This was mainly because he was always firm, fair and impartial. Johnson was a man of great self-discipline; his uniform was always impeccable. Johnson led by example; he worked very hard and expected the same of us. After a brief chat about the purpose of Sub Unit # 1 and what was expected of me, he sent me to find my bunking area.

I quickly fell into the routine of Sub Unit # 1. It was pleasant duty and we just did preventive maintenance of the equipment while waiting for the new battalion to come from Okinawa. We had to move every two to three months to a different battalion area, making us the nomads of the Division. Johnson turned out to be a great non-commissioned officer and he made the permanent members of Sub Unit #1 feel as if we were family. In addition to being a man of high integrity, Johnson was an excellent leader who always had a quick solution to all our problems. By now, I had had nearly two years as a private first class and when he found this out I was soon promoted to lance corporal.

In Sub Unit #1 I had picked up the nickname "Thumper" after Thumper Rabbit since my teeth looked like a rabbit's when I smiled. I liked the name and drew a rabbit on the back of my field jacket modeled after Nestlé's Quik cartoon bunny with the word "Thumper" across the top.

One of our favorite times in the sub unit was Johnson's Friday safety briefing before weekend liberty. We all found this very amusing. The Corps required it and Johnson tried to make it as amusing as possible. It went something like this: "You don't be driving down the road with those may-pop tires in your wreck of a car with your hand in the cunt of old Mary-Jane's crotch-rot. Don't get passionate while you're driving. If you are going to fuck, pull over to the side of the road and fuck, but don't try and drive and fuck at the same time! I want to see all you turds back here safe and ready for next week at the morning formation at 0700 hours Monday. Have a good weekend."

I was still meeting up with Clay and he would go home with me for the weekends from time to time. One day I got a call from Clay and he told me he was going to marry my sister Sue. Now I understood the attraction of going home with me! I told him that I thought it was good and he would be good for her. Clay had only signed up for three years active duty and would be going back to civilian life soon. Since I had a four-year active duty enlistment I had more than one and a half years left. Clay was looking forward to getting out and back to civilian life again.

As we were rotating battalions we moved from Camp Margarita to the other camps that housed the other regiments of the 1st Marine Division. I'm not sure at which camp it was but there was a time in 1964 when there was a great deal of racial tension and on one particular evening we were sitting in an outdoor theater watching a movie called the *The Victors*. It was a war movie trying to make a statement, trying to make a point: "War has no victors, only survivors. Killing destroys the killers as well as the killed!" The movie showed news clippings from WWII and then went to the battle front following a squad of American soldiers, showing the "true" story, which was not very pleasant. There was a scene in the movie toward the end where black troops in Paris were sitting in a night club enjoying themselves when a group of white soldiers busted into the club shouting we're "coon hunting." They ganged up and beat up the black soldiers. One of the black members of the audience shouted, "Those fucking chucks can't do that to a splib!" There was a great deal of anger in the audience from the black marines. We all went back to our barracks and after that we had groups of marauding black marines trying for several nights to find individual white marines to reverse the process. Racial tension was always just under the surface in the 1960s. It would flair up every once in a while. The scuttlebutt circulating about one of the battalions that we rotated back to Camp Pendleton was that there had been several deaths in race-related incidents in the battalion on Okinawa.

It was not that we were always at odds with each other as blacks and whites. I remember once at Camp San Onofre the sub unit took a Mighty Mite Jeep with a trailer and filled the trailer with ice. Blacks and whites who were members of Sub Unit #1 then put in several cases of beer. Camp San Onofre had one of the best beaches on the California coast just inside Camp Pendleton. We drove the Mighty Mite to the beach while the rest of Sub Unit # 1 rode to the beach party on two deuce and a half trucks (large open air trucks). Since the beach was inside the base we had it to ourselves. The sub unit had a great party without racial tension. It must be remembered that during 1964, Dr. Martin Luther King became the youngest person to receive the Nobel Peace Prize for his work to end racial segregation and racial discrimination, through civil disobedience and other nonviolent means. In Hong Kong these days, I often see black and white marines and sailors on liberty together. In my time of active duty, this would have been rare. I must say that the US military did far more to end racial segregation and racial discrimination than any other American institution. However, it was not a smooth process to go from a segregated armed service to an integrated one. In basic training Corporal Miller used to tell us, "You're all green now; there are no blacks or whites in my Marine Corps!"

Each battalion had its own special services program which provided recreational equipment for the members of the battalion. There was an occasion when three of us checked out bows and arrows. These were intended for archery target practice but we decided to go hunting with them. The arrows were target arrows and not designed for hunting. We had seen a lot of rabbits in the fields that surrounded the camp and split up to walk through the fields covering our own designated areas.

After about ten minutes I spotted a medium size rabbit sitting very quietly in a cactus patch about ten yards away. I drew the bow very carefully and shot at the rabbit and to my surprise hit him, pinning him to the ground. He did not move so I walked closer and shot the rabbit with another arrow. This time he let out a blood-curdling scream that gave me a horrible feeling and attracted my two friends. I shot another arrow and finally killed the rabbit. By then the friend who was the closest had run over and was looking at what had happened. My other friend arrived and asked, "What the fuck was that?" The friend who had been first on the scene lifted the rabbit by the arrows and said, "Thumper has killed one of his relatives." I was thinking that arrows are not good hunting weapons since they create no impact when they hit. Also, the arrows I was using were not designed for hunting so that could have had something to do with the rabbit surviving the first two. A rifle round, if from a high caliber rifle with enough power, would have hit very much harder! I felt the same hollow feeling that I had felt when I killed a squirrel as a child in Gulfport, but I held in my emotions.

On 2 August 1964, the first Gulf of Tonkin Incident took place. The destroyer USS *Maddox* was performing an intelligence gathering operation in the Gulf of Tonkin, when it was engaged by three North Vietnamese Navy torpedo boats of the 135th Torpedo Squadron, and a sea battle erupted. One US aircraft was damaged, one 14.5 mm round hit the destroyer, three North Vietnamese torpedo boats were damaged, four North Vietnamese sailors were killed and six were wounded; there were no US casualties.

The second Gulf of Tonkin Incident was supposed, for some years, to have taken place on 4 August 1964. However, it was revealed in 2005, in a declassified internal National Security Agency historical study, that there may not have been any North Vietnamese naval vessels present during the "incident" of 4 August 1964. It's ironic that the passage by Congress of the Gulf of Tonkin Resolution was based on this second incident, which may not actually have involved any North Vietnamese naval craft. The Gulf of Tonkin Resolution granted President Johnson the authority to assist any Southeast Asian country whose government was considered to be jeopardized by "communist aggression." This gave President Johnson the power to send armed service personnel to war without the permission of Congress.

It was sometime in late 1964 that I was promoted to corporal. Erastus Johnson gave me a very good performance rating since I enjoyed my work and toed the line for him. This was a big deal since it meant that I was an NCO. It also meant that I could wear the blood stripe (red stripe running down the seam of the trousers) on the trousers of my dress blues. You have to be an NCO or an officer to wear the blood stripe. It was a symbol of the many marine NCOs and officers who were killed in the Battle of Chapultepec during the Mexican-American war. It is also where the "from the Halls of Montezuma" line derives in the Marine Corps Hymn. Basically, in September 1847, marines stormed the castle of Chapultepec with great loss of officers and NCOs.

For us in Sub Unit #1, the Gulf of Tonkin Incident started the ball rolling in the direction of our becoming the beginnings of a new 3rd Battalion 5th Marines. Also, we were beginning to see that the Marines were being heavily committed to Vietnam. This was a surprise since up till 1964 we all figured that Laos was the place where we would be.

In the 1960s, a battalion landing team (BLT) was the basic Marine unit in an amphibious assault landing. It was a reinforced infantry battalion supported by additional combat and service elements. The reinforcements were usually a battery of artillery, a platoon of trucks (motor transport), tanks, amphibian tractors and a helicopter squadron. Additional personnel would include reconnaissance and engineers, and detachments of communications, beachmasters, and medical and logistical support. Although BLTs varied in size, the average strength was about 1,500 men, built around a Marine infantry battalion. On 8 March 1965, BLT 3/9 of the 9th Marine Expeditionary Brigade (MEB) did a landing northeast of Da Nang. Waiting for the marines on the beach were several welcoming South Vietnamese dignitaries and local schoolgirls who garlanded the 9th MEB commander, Brigadier General Frederick J. Karch, with flowers. This was highly publicized in the press at the time. BLT 3/9 was soon joined by BLT 1/9 in Da Nang; and by the end of March 1965, the 9th MEB had nearly 5,000 marines at Da Nang, including two infantry battalions, two helicopter squadrons and supporting units. The Marines had officially landed in Vietnam.

In Sub Unit # 1, we were wondering what effect this was going to have on us. We carried on in a normal manner until we were in the 3/5 area again and found out that we were not going to rotate another Okinawa battalion. The Okinawa platoons were going to stay in Southeast Asia. Instead we were going to be the beginnings of an H&S company for the newly formed 3rd Battalion 5th Marines.

CHAPTER EIGHTEEN

FORMING 3/5 FROM SUB UNIT #1

WE settled into the 3rd Battalion 5th Regiment (3/5) area of Camp Margarita. This time instead of just doing preventive maintenance on the equipment, we were going to own the equipment and be deployed as a full-strength battalion. We started to get the rest of the personnel to make up a full Headquarters and Services company and our new infantry battalion. We were starting to get our infantry line companies as well. A battalion would normally have an H&S company and four infantry line companies.

In the second half of 1965, we were initially offered a large re-enlistment bonus. I remember that for my military occupation specialty the amount was several thousand US dollars. I guess the planners could see trouble with not having enough non-commissioned officers to deal with the possible buildup in Vietnam and needed us to stay in the Corps. I know one of our sub unit corporals re-upped (signed another enlistment contract) and used the money to pay cash for a brand new Studebaker Avanti. It was a beautiful car and he thought it would give him great power over women, but we told him that just to buy a car was a stupid reason to commit for another four years. The re-up incentive did not attract most that were short (had little time left on their contract) to stay. We were then told that everyone's enlistment was to be extended involuntarily for 120 days. It seems that at that time, the Navy and Marine Corps' enlistment contracts had a provision for a four-month involuntary extension in case of a declared national emergency; and after the Gulf of Tonkin Incident, President Johnson had declared a state of emergency. This meant that I now had to serve until October 1966 instead of leaving active duty on 26 June 1966. The Corps needed to keep around as long as they could those of us who were experienced.

Soon after Sub Unit # 1 started to settle in to the 3/5 area, Johnson was reposted and our H&S Company gunny (gunnery sergeant) arrived. He was Gunny Chapman. We all thought that he looked like the TV cartoon character Deputy Dog. We never called him that to his face but we called him Deputy Dog among ourselves. Our new battalion commander was Lieutenant Colonel Bronars. For those of us in the communications platoon we received Captain Chalmers as our platoon commander. The coziness of being a small independent unit with no officers was quickly coming to an end. We were rapidly building into a fully fledged marine infantry battalion.

Lieutenant Colonel Bronars appointed a company commander for H&S; he was Captain Hans S. Haupt. I heard that Captain Haupt was a mustang. A mustang is a marine who had started in the enlisted ranks and later became a commissioned officer. This was usually the result of a battlefield commission for outstanding leadership on the field of battle. Normally, mustangs have a good understanding of being an enlisted man as well as an officer. I never personally knew Captain Haupt as I was down in the pecking order of H&S company, but I heard he was a hard-nosed, no-nonsense marine.

We started training to familiarize ourselves with the weapons that we would need when we went into Vietnam. It was like a less intense infantry training regiment course; really an ITR refresher course. In addition, we had our inoculations brought up to date. While doing my annual qualification on the rifle range I received four inoculations on the day before record day. It was hard dealing with the soreness in my arms and trying to get into the proper positions for firing my rifle.

We were taken to the M79 range and shot several shots each at an abandoned tank. The M79 is a shotgun type of grenade launcher and new to me; I had not seen it in ITR. It was a single-shot weapon and we had to reload after each time we fired.

The most memorable time was on the grenade range where we had to throw M61 hand grenades. The M61 has a filling of Composition B contained within a sheet-steel two-part outer shell. Under the outer cover was a pre-notched fragmentation coil inner liner. I was told that the notched inner core was a notched spring that was notched every quarter of an inch of a twelve-foot spring creating a large fragmentation pattern when the Composition B was detonated.

The grenade range had bunker-like throwing stations with a big pit in front. The pit had old tires in it and we were to try and throw the grenade so that it landed in the tire in front of our station. The sequence in the procedure was the command "pull pin" and we'd pull the pin from the grenade; "prepare to throw" and we pointed our free arm at the intended target and put the grenade-holding arm in the ready-to-throw position; then the command "throw" and we would throw and duck down into the bunker-like station and wait for the all-clear signal after all grenades had exploded.

When it was my group's turn I drew the extreme right station on the range. Being a left-hander, I was holding the grenade in my left hand when the instructor in my station said, "Corporal, put the grenade in your right hand." I said, "But sergeant..." Before I could finish, he cut me off and said, "Put the fucking grenade in your right hand." I did and said nothing more. We received the sequence of orders and finally "throw grenade." I threw the grenade and not only did I miss the tire, I missed the whole pit. The grenade rolled up next to a sign on the side of the pit. The range officer yelled in a panicky voice, "Hit the deck!" Everyone dropped to the ground. The grenades went off and mine caused a lot of dirt to fly over the bunkers. No one was hurt. The instructor yelled at me saying, "What the fuck is wrong with you, Corporal?" I smiled and said, "I tried to tell you I'm a left-hander." If I had drawn any other station, the grenade would have gone into the pit. It would not have hit my tire but at least it would have been in the pit.

As I walked back to the group down the hill smiling to myself, my friend Foley asked, "Was that you, Thumper?" I said, "Yeah, I blew the shit out of the range sign. That stubborn bastard of an instructor would not listen to me." I explained what had happened and they had a good laugh. I was put back in sequence to throw again and the next time I was allowed to use my left hand and got the grenade in the tire.

My mother was growing more and more uneasy as I was telling her about the buildup of 3/5 and by late 1965 it was apparent that we were soon going to be deployed overseas. Mom's maternal instincts wanted to protect her child. She was trying hard to figure out how to keep me from being deployed. She heard that our local congressional representative was in town to meet any of his constituents who were interested in hearing him speak. The open meeting was on a Friday night and I left Camp Margarita and arrived at home in time for my mother to drive us both to this meeting. We listened to his talk and afterwards Mom approached the congressman directly. She explained that I was due to be released from active duty in June 1966 and under my normal enlistment there was not enough time for me to be deployed. The congressman listened patiently and took notes. He told us that he would bring it up with the commandant of the Marine Corps.

To my surprise, two weeks later Mom received a letter from the congressman saying that he had spoken to the commandant of the Marine Corps about my case, but even though the commandant was sympathetic and understood my mother's concern he could not allow me to stay behind when my unit deployed because it would set a precedent. Mom went into a state of depression, but I assured her that I would be okay. The truth was I wanted to go overseas and was happy to hear that the commandant was not going to grant Mom her wish.

The big news of December 1965 was that Gemini 6 and 7 had met up high above the Earth. The Astronauts proved that two spaceships could meet in almost the same orbit and that humans could survive for the time needed to get to the moon and back. The US was still going strong to keep President Kennedy's promise to put a man on the moon before the 1960s were out. In Vietnam, US planes began flying combat missions over South Vietnam. On the ground, 23,000 American advisors were now committed to combat roles. While we were still Sub Unit #1, some of the overseas returning members of the casual section were telling us about being advisors in Vietnam.

As for me, Christmas of 1965 and New Year of 1966 came and went with me on leave at home with my family. Then the month of January was spent preparing for deployment.

CHAPTER NINETEEN

TRANSPORT SHIP TO OKINAWA

WE boarded the USS *Renville* On 3 February 1966 at Long Beach, California, on route to Okinawa. The *Renville* was a little younger than me. She was launched on 25 October 1944 and commissioned as the USS *Renville* (APA-227) on 15 November 1944. After WWII, she was decommissioned on 30 June 1949 at Mare Island Naval Shipyard, Vallejo, California. The ship was then laid up in the Pacific Reserve Fleet until she was recommissioned on 5 January 1952 for the Korean War. Since then and at the time when we boarded her she had been in continual active service.

Once on board the *Renville*, I was assigned to the forward troop hold. My bunk was on the starboard side of the ship close to the bow. As we got underway we soon learned that we were in a convoy of three ships.

As we were sailing, I realized that you can hear the bow wake rushing along the outside of the ship's steel plates. As normal, when we first boarded and were underway, we had to have an abandon-ship drill. This was a very frustrating exercise as we had to get our life jackets on and make our way to our assigned lifeboat. Down in the troop hold of the *Renville* waiting for our turn to go on deck was a sickening experience. The ship was rolling and many marines were seasick. Someone had vomited in the water fountain, others were holding their helmets and vomiting in them. The smell made nearly everyone seasick.

After a day or so, life got into a routine. Living on a troop transport ship is very trying. The bunks were six high, six-feet long and had about eighteen inches of space for the occupant. I had taken a bunk on the bottom, which was a mistake since many men were seasick and would lie in their bunks and vomit. During the day, a marine's sea bag and all his gear had to rest on the bunk. There was a bar at the back of the bunk to lock your M14 to. In the daylight hours, marines would huddle all over the decks trying to find a place to spend time. At night, the passageways between bunks were made into mountains of sea bags and gear. Being on the bottom bunk, it was sometimes a problem climbing out over all the sea bags and gear to go to the head.

Most of the time at sea was spent in chow lines. We were assigned colored chow passes to keep order as people would file to the mess deck to eat. You would hear "yellow chow pass to the port side" on the ship PA system. If you had a yellow chow pass you would go to the left side of the ship and line up in this never-ending line. The chow lines were a place to read a book or chat to a fellow marine to kill time until it was your turn to eat. Once on the mess deck, you would take your metal tray and be served the meal. To occupy our time between chow lines we were having Vietnamese language and culture classes or PT on the fantail of the ship. The classes were conducted by people who had read a book or had been in "Nam" before as an advisor. The only thing that stuck was the word "deedee" which meant "go away." Very handy when surround by Vietnamese trying to sell you drinks or kids trying to see what they could get from you.

Our PT was limited because of lack of space but we mostly did exercises such as pushups. On the way down we would shout "kill" on the way up it was "VC". The system had started to psych us up for combat.

We were at sea for nine days before stopping in Hawai'i. One of the three ships in the convoy blew a boiler and we had to slow down. I remember seeing the island of Oahu at sunrise on the ninth day with cloud cover over the mountains. The famous landmark of Diamond Head was barely visible due to the limited light of dawn but was still a spectacular sight. As we sailed on, the street lights on Saint Louis Heights were still illuminated and the mountains of Oahu were a welcome sight after nine days on the ocean. Approaching Pearl Harbor, the water went from a deep blue (almost black) to turquoise and then to a green color, signaling that the water was getting shallower.

After we docked, word was sent around that we had to go over the side of the ship on cargo nets into landing craft. This seemed like a keep-busy exercise since the water in Pearl Harbor was as smooth as a lake. There is no experience like trying to step off a cargo net and seeing the floor of the landing craft you are trying to board drop five or six feet due to a swell. In port, boarding landing craft was not a realistic exercise. The only excitement was that it was carried out in a shower of rain.

After the landing craft exercise I caught the bus from Pearl Harbor to downtown Honolulu by myself. In later years, when I moved to Honolulu to live, I realized that I had got off the bus in the famous River Street area, a very bad district of Honolulu. The place looked very dirty and I walked around Honolulu until I came to a better area and found Saint Andrew's Cathedral. The cathedral is a very impressive building with a high ceiling and beautiful stained glass windows. I soon grew tired of walking around and of being approached by dubious people and hitchhiked back to the *Renville* at Pearl Harbor.

Our stopover in Honolulu was short-lived and we were soon underway again. It was a little disappointing that we did not get more time in Hawai'i. The next stretch of ocean from Hawai'i to Okinawa took far more than nine days. Life returned to the routine of ship life, with the mountain of sea bags at night, chow lines, PT, classes, and day after day looking at the vast open sea.

Sometimes at night, while on deck, you could see the wake of the ship stirring up little phosphorescent organisms that glowed and made the ship look as if it was sailing on a carpet made up of stars. The first time I saw this phenomenon it blew my mind.

Every few days, a little island could be seen just on the horizon, normally given away by a cover of cloud. Islands normally attract clouds so if you see a cloud bank at sea it could be over an island. There were a couple of days when we had very high seas. The ship pitched and rolled making many people seasick. I was on deck when the ship's bow went through a giant swell washing the decks clear up to the bridge.

After about ten days from our Hawaiian stopover I was getting my chow and had a glass of milk as usual. I was surprised to find it had a funny taste. I then learned that the milk had been UHT treated to be able to make the voyage. The ultra-high temperature process is like a super pasteurization but leaves the milk with a strange taste. Overseas we were never given fresh milk and I craved it.

As a corporal, I was once assigned duty to supervise the cleaning of our troop hold. I duly supervised the process of cleaning and swabbing the cabin soles and waited for the inspection. I don't know what was found but the shit hit the fan! I was scolded for the troop hold's condition. Being a corporal is an unfortunate position. You are not accepted by the sergeants and looked upon with suspicion by the lower ranks. I was sitting in the mess hall with a group of fellow corporals when one of the newly promoted sergeants came in and chewed out my ass again about the field day (the major cleaning of an area). As he left, I remember one of my fellow corporals – I think it was Foley – said, "You should not have taken that shit; you should have kicked his ass." Good in theory, but it could lead to some time in the brig and a ship's brig is not appealing. I was not assigned duty to supervise the field day of the troop hold for the rest of the voyage.

There was a rumor that there had been a secret inspection where one of the sergeants went though the troop holds with a flash light and found rust on a marine's M14 and that the owner of the M14 was promptly put into the brig. I don't know if this was rumor or fact, but it did not help the morale of the troops.

One Sunday, for entertainment, we had a smoker. The top of a cargo hold was roped off to make a boxing ring and there was a full afternoon of boxing matches. In the few days before the matches, the marines and sailors who were to box practised on deck. The smoker started with the "grudge" matches. If you had a grudge about someone this was the time to have it out. The very first match was between two squids (sailors) and there was no love lost between them. One of the squids lost his temper and tried to kick and throw the other squid out of the ring. In the end, the squid who had taken the most punishment won due to the dirty tactics of the other.

Our doc – paramedic corpsmen in the Marines are navy corpsmen who wear a Marine uniform with naval rank and are called doc – surprised everyone when he knocked out his opponent in about ten seconds. Later, we found out that he had done some amateur boxing prior to joining the navy.

We arrived at White Beach, Okinawa, on a rainy morning. We disembarked and were loaded into buses to be transported to Camp Schwab. I remember the excitement of being on Okinawa, my first overseas assignment.

CHAPTER TWENTY

OKINAWA

I had been in the Marines since June 1962 but had never left California. We jokingly used to say, "Join the Marines and see foreign lands and meet new and interesting people and kill them." I had done none of these and maybe did not wish to do all of them but I did want to see the world. It was a great feeling going along the road to Camp Schwab looking at the strange new sights through a bus window wet by the rain. I was surprised that trees looked just like trees in the US! I sat in the bus watching the scenery through the rain with a very warm and happy feeling. The countryside of Okinawa was foreign to me, but it still looked very welcoming. It was a very green island with mountains.

We arrived at Camp Schwab, finding it in a beautiful location with a scenic bay behind the barracks. There was a local village right outside the gate of Camp Schwab called Henoko. Okinawa was the next step in molding us into an integrated infantry battalion and eventually a battalion landing team. Camp Schwab was to be our home for a little over a month.

We settled in very quickly to the local environment. Henoko had a few bars and a great karate dojo. For some reason I did not go into Henoko very often. I only went to the local karate dojo a couple of times with a friend who was seriously studying karate. During my stay in Okinawa I only drank in town once after a karate lesson.

One of my favorite liberty calls was a weekend skosh cab (small cab) ride down to Koza city. The skosh cab drivers would fly down the road taking corners as if they were Grand Prix aces. We jokingly called them "kamikaze drivers." Kadena Air Base was in Koza and several of my friends and I loved to go to the non-commissioned officers' club at Kadena. For a reasonable price I could get a great filet mignon that was cooked by wrapping it in a strip of bacon served with vegetables and a baked potato. This was a special treat and we could not get anything like it in the NCO club at Camp Schwab. The US Air Force sure knew how to live. It seemed as if they were not in the military but more like in a great civilian job with extra comforts.

I ate in the town of Koza a couple of times but we were warned not to eat the local green vegetables or drink the local milk. We were told that farmers in the area used human manure to fertilize the vegetables. They had "honey buckets" that they would use to carry the human waste to the fields every morning. Also, there was in Koza what were called "benjo ditches," sewers that were partially open. As you walked down the streets the smell of sewage filled the air. Okinawa's residents did not seem to mind it.

Despite the warnings, I ate the green vegetables and as I had such a great craving for fresh milk I drank the local milk at the restaurants. It was far better than the UHT milk we were getting at Camp Schwab. I was overseas and wanted to experience the local culture.

In Koza, we would go to a local massage parlor and get a steam bath and massage. The ladies who did the massaging were middle-aged women and were very stout and strong. They could get our muscles back in order very quickly, especially after some time in the field when our muscles were sore from hiking. However, I could never get used to the bath that was given prior to the massage. You first sat on a stool and were washed from head to toe by these ladies and then spent time in a hot tub soaking. I felt that something was wrong having an old lady bathing me as if I were a child.

Also, we found the brothels in Koza very quickly. Brothels are more efficient than bars since you eliminate the ritual of talking and buying drinks and pretending that the girl loves you. We learned of their whereabouts from the marines who had been stationed on Okinawa before. Okinawa did not have the same feel as Mexico. It was more developed and had a very different culture. Since I did not go into Henoko often, I could not compare the bar life of Okinawa to Tijuana.

The culture on Okinawa was Japanese with an Okinawan flavor. The Okinawan people did not have the same sense of modesty when it came to using the toilet. In our barracks we had a line of about eight toilets, side by side in the open and about two feet apart. There were civilians hired to work on the base. One day I was sitting on a toilet in the barracks when an older Okinawan woman worker came in and sat on a toilet several down from me. She politely looked at me and bowed while sitting and said, "Ohayou gozaimasu." I was totally surprised and did a slight bow in return.

On 5 April 1966, some of our line company marines, along with some of our communications platoon men, went to board the USS *Whitfield County* at Naha and sailed for Japan. They disembarked at Numasu Beach, Japan, on 6 April 1966 and spent ten days at Mount Fuji. This was a cold-weather training area for the Corps. I understand that during their time there they went to the rifle range. They returned to Camp Schwab by ship after their training.

At around the same time, a group of our radio operators went to the Philippines for training. I believe they went to practice calling in air and naval gun-fire. I remember one of my friends, Foley, telling us of a monkey which took a roll of their toilet paper up a tree in their campsite then unwrapped and tangled it in the tree tops. He said that he shot it with his .45. I stayed on Okinawa and went to the northern training area for a few days. I was envious since I would have loved to go to Mount Fuji or the Philippines.

Later I and others in Headquarters and Service Company had to go to the rifle range to get our "combat sights." We fired from prone at 300 yards. When we were sighted in, we painted a white line across the sight adjustments that we used. This way, if we ever hit our sight we could align the white line on the sight adjustments and we would have our combat sights again that were sighted in for 300 yards.

The whole H&S Company had to go to the northern training area in late April 1966. During our training we did live fire by walking up a stream as a squad, and as pop-up targets appeared we had to shoot them from the hip.

We had to learn how to cross three types of rope bridge. The one-strand bridge was crossed by pulling ourselves across the top of the single rope as if we were crawling on the ground. We lay on the rope with one leg on the rope to push and we would pull with our hands. The two- and three-strand bridges were much easier to cross. The two-strand bridge was crossed by side-stepping on the bottom rope and using the top rope with our hands. The three-strand bridge was crossed by walking on the bottom rope and holding on to the other two ropes on either side. The three-strand bridge was by far the easiest to cross.

We were then taught how to rappel down a rock face. We were shown how to make a harness with rope and how to control the speed of decent down the rock by braking with the rope.

The final activity was one that was designed so that everyone had to get wet. It was called the "slide for life." A thick steel cable ran from a platform on the top of a high cliff to a tree at the bottom. The cable went over the tops of the trees below the cliff and then over a river. The cable was at a fairly steep angle and had a wheel with a handle attached beneath it, which you held on to as the wheel slid down the cable. There was someone at the bottom of the slide with a flag who would signal to you when to let go and fall into the river. This day the flag man was our doc. He would wave the flag and you would hold your legs out straight, let go of the handle, land in the water and skim across the surface to stop. The joke was that since you were going so fast when you hit the water it was like having an enema. If you froze up and did not let go you would hit the tree at the bottom at a very high speed. We were told that we did not have to go on it if we did not want to. However, I did not see a single marine decline going down the slide. It came to my turn and I stepped off the platform, but somehow as I did so I turned backwards. I was looking up at the platform as I screamed across the tops of the trees. I was trying hard to look over my shoulder to see the flag signal. Luckily, I slowly turned around on the cable and was facing the signal man when he dropped the flag. I felt the water as I skidded across the surface, slowing down. The flag man, our doc, ran over to me shouting, "Thumper, you dumb fuck, only you would go down the slide for life backwards."

As we got closer to the time we were to leave Okinawa, a different feeling came over 3/5. Foley and I were in the NCO club a few nights before we were to sail and several fights broke out. Some people ended up throwing their glasses across the club. Our H&S mortar platoon came back from the E-club (for enlisted men) marching in formation and got into a brawl with one of the line companies when they marched past the line company's barracks making a noise.

On the last few evenings, I went out by the bay and sat by myself watching the ocean and listening to the small waves lapping onto the shore. It was peaceful and a great relief from the tension in camp. Even though I was not religious, I started to talk to God aloud. I asked God for courage to deal with what I was about to encounter. I guess that the religion that was instilled in me by my grandparents was still somewhere in my subconscious. Going to war is something that is hard to describe. I wanted to go in-country but deep inside me my upbringing was against killing another human being. All my training for the last four years was to kill or to support killing. It was a big paradox.

CHAPTER TWENTY-ONE

OKINAWA TO SUBIC BAY

ON 11 May 1966, those of us in Headquarters and Service Company boarded the USS *Princeton*, designated as LPH-5 (Landing Platform Helicopter-5) in Okinawa. The *Princeton* was to be our home for the next few months. We were a special landing force (SLF), designated Battalion Landing Team (BLT) 3/5, and in addition to the *Princeton* there were marines from 3/5 aboard two other ships, the USS *Alamo* and the USS *Pickaway*. We were joined by our reinforcements and – apart from not having our helicopters – we were now a BLT.

The *Alamo* LSD-33, as a landing ship dock, was to transport and launch amphibious craft and vehicles with their crews and other marines for the amphibious operations we were about to undertake. She was the youngest of the three ships in the SLF. Construction on her started on 11 October 1954 at Pascagoula, Mississippi, by the Ingalls Shipbuilding Corporation; she was launched on 20 January 1956 and commissioned on 24 August 1956. The *Alamo*'s displacement was 8,899 tons. Her length was 510 feet, and she had a beam of 84 feet and a draft of 19 feet. The *Alamo* had a top speed of 21 knots and was not as fast as the *Princeton*. Her crew had a complement of 304 and could accommodate 300 marines. The *Alamo* had a well deck and could carry twenty-one LCM (landing craft mechanized) 6s. In addition she could accommodate up to eight helicopters.

The *Pickaway* APA-222 was an attack transport ship and was used as a troop carrier. The *Pickaway* was constructed by the Permanente Metals Corporation, Richmond, California. She was launched as a victory cargo ship on 5 November 1944. She was acquired by the US Navy and commissioned on 12 December 1944 as an APA. She had a displacement of 14,837 tons, a length of 455 feet, a beam of 62 feet and a draft of 24 feet. Her top speed was 18 knots.

The *Princeton*, the flag ship of the SLF, was the fifth *Princeton* in the US Navy, originally laid down as the *Valley Forge* at the Philadelphia Navy Yard on 14 September 1943. The ship was renamed the *Princeton* on 21 November 1944 and launched on 8 July 1945 as CV-37 (aircraft carrier), making the

Princeton just a few months younger than me. She had been put in mothballs between WWII and the Korean War. After being recommissioned she won a highly decorated battle record during the Korean War.

The *Princeton* was an impressive sight. She displaced 33,000 tons, her length was 888 feet with a beam of 93 feet (extreme width at flight deck: 147½ feet), and her draft was 28 feet 7 inches. She could do 33 knots, which was mind-boggling for a mass of metal so large. The *Princeton* went through several classifications as an aircraft carrier during her service. Finally, on 2 March 1959, the *Princeton* was converted and reclassified from an aircraft carrier to an LPH-5. From this last conversion the *Princeton* had emerged as an amphibious assault carrier. Basically, she was reconfigured to transport a Marine battalion landing team and carried helicopters in place of planes. The ship had a wooden flight deck and the length of the deck must have been too short for 1960s naval combat aircraft.

After boarding, we sailed toward Subic Bay in the Philippines. Sailing on the *Princeton* had its similarities and differences from the *Renville*, the ship that had taken us from California to Okinawa. The *Princeton* was so big it seemed like a floating island. It did not pitch and roll as the *Renville* had done when we crossed the Pacific. The advantage of the *Princeton* was that there was a lot more room as she was a carrier. However, ship life was similar. We had troop bunking areas that were cramped and we had a similar chow pass procedure. We settled down to a marine's structured ship life again very quickly.

One activity that I had never done much of before ship life was to read. On board ship I had discovered books to kill time. At Camp Pendleton there were books, but they tended to be great literary works such as *Fanny Hill*. The more commonly found books on ships were lesser literary works that held together with little plot and very descriptive accounts of sexual encounters. They were affectionately referred to by us as "fuck books." The joke was that if you dropped a fuck book it automatically opened at the right pages. I started to read on the *Renville* and now went back to books as a way of dealing with ship life on the *Princeton*. On the trip over from California on the *Renville* I read *Crime and Punishment*, which was a great ship book since it was so long. The Russian novel was designed for the long Russian winters and ship's life for marines had its time similarities to Russian winters.

On the *Princeton*, I had now started on *Catch 22*, which seemed appropriate for a person about to go in-country. A fellow marine – the karate practitioner I had been to the Henoko dojo with – started to give some of us karate lessons on the hanger deck.

I had made friends with the squids who were running the ship's radio relay room. The relay room was on the ship's bridge and it was air conditioned. The great thing was that the squids would allow several of us to sleep there in our sleeping bags, which was far better than the cramped non-air-conditioned troop quarters. Several friends and I had befriended one of the Recon Marines who were attached to us and we would hang out on the catwalks below the flight deck. The catwalks were great since you were well above the water, and could watch the ship cut through the waves far below. Not only this, but it was cool with tons of fresh air. On the catwalk, we would "shoot the shit" (talk about anything) and play chess. We had to find ways to entertain ourselves since ship life for a marine was boring. Our work was waiting on shore in Vietnam, but until then we were only human cargo.

We arrived in the Philippines on the tail of a typhoon. This was the only time I felt the *Princeton* pitch and roll. Since she was so big, the roll was a very slow, sickening roll compared to the *Renville*. On 20 May 1966, in the morning, we slowly steamed into Subic Bay and dropped anchor. We could not tie up at the main pier that was designed for aircraft carriers, since the USS *Ranger* was already there. It was an exciting feeling being in the Philippines as we had heard so much about Olongapo from the old salts.

That afternoon we were given liberty for the first time. We had to be ferried to land by liberty boats. After getting off the boat, I passed a restaurant on the base on the way into town called the Spanish Gate. The Spanish Gate was very close to the main dock where carriers tied up and it became a regular spot for most of us on the way to and from liberty. To get into Olongapo you had only to follow the crowd. There was a stream of sailors and marines making their way to the main gate with money in their pockets to spend on a good time.

The main gate of Subic Bay was before a bridge that crossed over a drainage channel that we referred to as "Shit River." The scuttlebutt was that the US Navy had analyzed the water in the channel and it was only slightly cleaner than human shit. From the bridge, you could toss coins for young kids to dive for in the murky, smelly water. It was amazing how they could see to retrieve the coins. On the other side of the bridge was the great city of Olongapo.

As you started to cross the bridge to enter into Olongapo, the first big landmark was a large structure that dominated the view; this was the cock fighting arena. I never went to a cock fight but there was a great story about a group of our officers who went there. One young lieutenant, who was very drunk, got into a heated discussion with a squid. The squid punched him in the stomach causing the young officer to vomit all over the squid, thus quickly ending the altercation.

On the Olongapo side of the bridge was Magsaysay Drive. Olongapo – and Magsaysay Drive in particular – were the wildest places on Earth that I had ever visited. Up until my first visit to Olongapo I held the opinion that Tijuana was the sin capital of the world. On my first day in Olongapo I had to reclassify my repertoire of known sin capitals and put Olongapo at the top of the list.

Walking down Magsaysay Drive by myself, taking in the environment, I met a squid whom I befriended for the day. We introduced ourselves to each other and went through the usual ritual of: "What ship are you on? What state are you from? What city? How long have you been in the military?" etc. It seemed that once this basic set of information had been exchanged it was as if we had been lifelong friends. As young servicemen on liberty, friendships are made and dropped very rapidly. I never met this young man again nor do I remember his name, but for the day we were the best of friends.

The squid was a real Olongapo raider and was keen to take me on a tour to show off his knowledge of my newly found sin capital. We started to visit the various bars along the strip having one San Miguel beer at each bar. In the Philippines in those days, the only beer available was San Miguel. On the street's sidewalk there was meat being charcoal-barbequed on hibachis. I enquired of my new friend what kind of meat it was and he said with a smile on his face, "Monkey meat." Of course being a little drunk I had to try it. It was nothing special. By now we had drunk a few San Miguels and he wanted to introduce me to a good bar he knew. We had to take a jeepney to this great establishment. We ended up a long way down from the main gate in a place named the Bay View.

The Bay View bar was two stories high with a sitting bar downstairs and a sitting bar with tables and a dance floor upstairs. The mamasan was a large, middle-aged woman called Mama Rosita. I was told she was referred to as "Mama Rosita and the twin 45s." The twin 45s referred to the mamasan's breasts, which were unusually enormous for a Philippine woman.

As in most bars in Olongapo, it was full of lovely young Philippine women who were looking to drink, dance or whatever else that was needed with young servicemen, for a fee of course. Normally, the girls would get commission on the drinks bought for them and if you took one of them to any of the small hotels for a short time, a bar fine had to be paid. The fee for the service had to be negotiated with the girl prior to services being provided and the bar fine was separate.

We had taken a table upstairs overlooking the dance floor and started to drink our San Miguel beers. By now my squid friend was working on, "rapping a line", as we would say in the Marines, to a young woman for whom he had bought a drink. I'm sure he must have known her from another occasion since they were on a first name basis without any introductions.

There was a lovely young woman sitting at the bar who winked at me. My friend switched his concentration from his woman friend for a moment to tell me: "The woman that winked at you is Marilyn; she is a great fuck." The next thing I knew Marilyn was sitting with us and I had bought her a drink. It seems that my friend had planned to end his liberty with the Bay View woman all along. However, it was nice of him to kill time with me in showing me the town. He shook hands with me and disappeared with his woman. I could not blame him since he was shipping out the next day.

As a young, twenty-one-year-old marine who had been at sea for a few days, the sight of a young, shapely, good-looking woman was too much to resist. I soon learned the rules of bar fines and where there was a convenient hotel room. We became instant friends, as one would in these circumstances.

Back aboard ship we exchanged stories about our liberty and it seems as if my story about the Bay View attracted a following. The next day several of us communications (Comms) types took the jeepney ride to the Bay View. I was greeted by Marilyn and my fellow marines made friends with their own Philippine beauties very quickly. For the next two nights this became a ritual.

On our first night together as a Comms group at the Bay View we discovered the bar made a drink called a Mojo that was served in a pitcher. The drink tasted like Kool-Aid but with a kick like a mule from its high alcohol content. I do not know the Bay View's recipe for a Mojo but I found several recipes on the internet. The following example will indicate the power of the mixture: 1 bottle of beer; 5 shots dark rum; 5 shots vodka; 5 shots gin; 5 shots whisky; 4 oz of pineapple juice; 4 oz of orange juice; 4 oz of 7-Up; 1 shot of lime juice; dash of grenadine; 5 pieces of calamansi or 1 lemon.

I would imagine that this is a close approximation to the Bay View's drink. However, I remember seeing the bartender pouring a small bottle of rum into the pitcher and think the Bay View Mojo might have had a small bottle of dark rum and a small bottle of light rum in place of the vodka, gin and whiskey, plus shots of rum and the addition of a Cola. I'm sure that the recipe varied from bar to bar.

As young marines, we decided that what we needed was a Mojo drinking contest. The rules were very simple, everyone stood and each participant had a glass full of Mojo from the pitcher. On signal we would all chug the glass of Mojo. Glasses were set back on the table and all those who remained standing would have their glass filled again. Some would lose interest and leave with a young woman to do whatever. The procedure was repeated until only one marine was left standing. The winner was given a little garland of flowers made from sweet-smelling local blossoms. After finishing a Mojo contest, as we used to say in the Marines, "you couldn't find your own ass with your own hands."

CHAPTER TWENTY-TWO

OPERATION HILLTOP AND JUNGLE SURVIVAL TRAINING

THERE were a number of Operation Hilltops and I believe ours was designated Operation Hilltop VI. Operation Hilltop was the last exercise of a battalion landing team before going into action in-country in Vietnam. No matter what the Operation Hilltop designation was, we were on our way to our first trial integrated operation to prepare us for special landing force operations in Vietnam.

For us on the *Princeton*, Operation Hilltop began in Subic Bay. Personnel from Headquarters and Service Company, who were to set up the command post (CP) on combat operations, first worked with the Red Lions, our Marine Air Unit HMM-363 (Helicopter Marine Medium-363), which used H-34 Seahorse helicopters. This took place on the morning of 24 May 1966. HMM-363 had been aboard the *Princeton* for only three days. Our line companies on the other two ships had left the previous day for Mindoro aboard the *Alamo* and *Pickaway*. They were to do a traditional landing on the beach for the line company side of the amphibious assault.

The helicopters that had been sitting on the flight deck and in the hanger deck for the previous three days were a mystery but were soon to become very familiar to us. In 1966, the H-34 was the Marine Corps workhorse; it was initially developed by Sikorsky Aircraft as a private development, which the military ignored. After its development, the Marines adopted the H-34 as the Seahorse and it was affectionately labeled "the dog" by marine helicopter pilots and crew of the day. Once in service, the H-34 was soon adopted by other armed services both in the US and abroad. The US Army called it the Choctaw. However, while I was in Vietnam the army was already using the Bell UH-1 series Iroquois – better known as the Huey – as their workhorse.

The H-34 had a rotor diameter of 17.7 meters (56 ft), a length of 14.7 meters (46 ft 9 in) and a height of 4.8 meters (15 ft 11 in). It was powered by a nine-cylinder air-cooled Wright R-1820-84 reciprocating engine that turned the single rotor. The engine was massive and required a very elaborate blower system to keep it cool. The H-34's shaft and gearbox were situated along the spine of the fuselage and a very large tail pylon drove the tail rotor. To save weight, the fuselage of the H-34 was all magnesium alloy metal. The interior of the Seahorse was empty of seats and marines had to sit on the floor of the helicopter to be transported. The chopper was an impressive sight when you started to board since it was so tall.

We started Operation Hilltop by boarding an H-34 chopper from the deck of the *Princeton* and flying to the large island of Mindoro, just south of Manila in the curved part of Luzon. This was my first helicopter ride and I found the trip very exciting, especially sitting on the deck with no seat belts. We were at the mercy of the pilot's skill to keep us in the H-34. As we left the deck of the *Princeton*, we could soon see all of Subic Bay and it was a great sight. The ocean, tropical jungle and mountains of the Philippines were spectacular. It was like something out of a movie.

We flew over to the center of Mindoro and left the chopper in a mountainous area. We walked through a small village and were the center of attention. I guess that there is not much excitement in the boondocks of Mindoro and the arrival of a group of US Marines was newsworthy in such a quiet place.

We set up our CP and settled into life in the field on the top of a hill that had a fairly steep slope. It started to rain, off and on. I believe that we were still being affected by the end of the typhoon that we had experienced on our arrival at Subic. The rain was not good and at the end of the first day on Mindoro I felt as if my whole body was wrinkled up like a prune from being constantly wet!

The next couple of nights were very eventful. As evening fell and the rain subsided, the locals came around and were very friendly. I retired to my poncho tent only to be called out a couple of hours later. The local men had taken a liking to our generator; there was no electricity in the mountains and they decided that they were going to take our generator for their village. This was supposed to be an operation to prepare us for Vietnam, but we never anticipated this. The locals had drunk a little too much San Miguel and were in an aggressive mood. We had our M14 rifles but no ammo. We fixed our bayonets and grouped together to give ourselves a no-nonsense appearance. One of the locals threw an empty San Miguel bottle at us then the whole group of around ten men started to throw their bottles as well. In retaliation, we ended up throwing rocks and their empty bottles back at them. Seeing our fixed bayonets they decided that it would be foolish to attack us, so they retreated for the night.

The rain continued and life was generally miserable. The next evening the rain let up for a little while and again we had local visitors. As I was trying to sleep in my tent someone came close to the fabric and said in a whisper, "Do you want young girl? Only ten US dollars! She is a virgin; she is my daughter!" My whole body was like a prune and I had lost the feeling in my left foot by now. Generally speaking, I was not in the mood for having a woman in the tent. Also, I was deeply infatuated with my new-found friend, Marilyn, and my only desire was to get back to her. However, my tent mate asked, "Can I see her?" I riposted, saying, "You must be joking! You can't bang a whore in this tent." He declined the man's offer and we tried to get to sleep since it was not raining for a change.

At the end of Operation Hilltop we boarded the chopper and flew back to the *Princeton*. Getting aboard ship was a great feeling. After returning to the *Princeton* we were given liberty, which we took advantage of by visiting our girlfriends at the Bay View, holding Mojo drinking contests and so on.

After a couple of days, it was now time for us to do our jungle survival training. I understand that you can have a jungle survival course that lasts up to seven days. We were to get an abbreviated two-day version designed for the infantry. The seven-day course was specifically for pilots in case they got shot down. The US military used the nearby mountains to train its forces in jungle fighting and survival.[2] Our teachers were the

---

[2] After the US returned Subic Bay to the Philippines, the Jungle Environment Survival Training (JEST) program was set up and converted what had been the military's jungle survival training into a budding enterprise by combining environmental awareness and tourism, as "eco-tourism." Many years later, on a sailing trip from Hong Kong to Puerto Galera on the island of Mindanao, we stopped at Subic Bay. I asked about the JEST program and was told that many tourists now paid good money to go on the course.

aboriginal Aetas or Negritos who had lived in the forest for generations and understood it well.

We left the *Princeton* and hiked to the training venue, which was a few miles into the jungle area of the base and was said to be a Philippine national forest. We carried a minimal amount of gear since we were not setting up a CP, and very few rations. It was extremely hot and humid on the hike up, and it did not get much better when we got out of the direct sunlight and into the jungle. Most of us were soaked, headachy, fatigued and on the verge of heat stroke.

We had two instructors who were middle-aged men of tiny stature. They were very much at home in the jungle. Both carried the machete-type knife of the Philippines, which is called a bolo. Generally the bolos were made of sharpened car springs.

The first thing that we were shown was the construction of a raised sleeping platform; it was quickly constructed from material growing around us: bamboo, rattan vines, banana leaves, fashioned with their sharp bolo knifes. We were then shown vines that, when cut, will give you water. They showed us some edible plants, a few medicinal plants and how to twist vines to make a rope.

As evening approached, the two instructors showed us how to dam a stream, find fresh water snails and catch small fish with our bare hands. One of the instructors cut a large section of a big, green, bamboo stalk. Bamboo has sections that are sealed and will hold water. He then sliced a wedged-shaped section out of the top to create a bamboo cooking utensil. The instructor then started a fire with no matches and put a handful of rice, some water, a few snails and a couple of small fish inside the newly formed bamboo cooking pot. The wedge was put back in place and the whole thing put in the fire with the cut wedge facing up to keep the water from spilling. When the rice was done, he split off the top half of the bamboo and we proceeded to have dinner. At the end of the meal, they threw the empty bamboo cooking utensil into the fire using it as fire wood.

By the evening I was in bad shape. I had contracted diarrhea and was vomiting up everything including water. Our instructors were very resourceful and as if by magic had somehow come up with a case of San Miguel with ice – and a guitar. They were busy serenading the troops, while I felt like death warmed up and was not appreciative of the entertainment. After everyone retired to their two-man poncho tents I finally fell asleep.

I woke up with the most ungodly cramps and took my entrenching tool (small shovel) out to dig myself a cat-hole to deal with the next bout of diarrhea that was building up pressure in my guts. I stepped out of the tent and felt a great urge to relieve myself and started to drop my utility pants. As I got them around my knees and was bent over forward I could not hold on any longer and shot out a stream of diarrhea that must have gone four meters down the hill. Luckily, I was facing away from the tent with my posterior and there were no tents behind me, otherwise it would have been a mess.

The next morning we hiked back to the *Princeton* with me very dehydrated and in a bad way. However, I was a corporal and was not going to show that I was weak! The nausea had in fact disappeared and I was starting to feel a little better.

Once on the *Princeton*, we showered and changed for liberty. My strength was returning rapidly with the thought of spending time with Marilyn. My bar pack of marines and I made our way to the Bay View.

CHAPTER TWENTY-THREE

FINAL DAYS PRIOR TO DECKHOUSE 1

WE knew that we would sail on the morning of 8 June 1966. On the day before sailing all those of us who were granted liberty went into town around noon for our last hurrah. As usual, Marilyn and I spent the early afternoon in one of the short-time hotels along Magsaysay Drive. By going there prior to her reporting for duty we avoided paying the bar fine.

We went for our final meal together in a small restaurant before I shipped out; I was devastated that I was going to be leaving her for a few weeks. We ate very early when it was still light outside and I had a hamburger washed down with a few San Migs. I missed the hamburgers of my home in California; the Philippine hamburger was not up to my expectations. After eating, we made our way back to the Bay View bar since Marilyn was on duty. When we arrived at the Bay View a group from the communications platoon was well into the traditional Mojo drinking contest. Other shipmates were spending the time with their new girlfriends as I was doing, trying to make the best of a bad situation. Marilyn and I went to the upper-floor dance floor, which was already alive with sailors and marines dancing with their women to jukebox music. The Bay View had a good selection of late 50s to the newest 1966 hits.

Marilyn and I selected a table on the Bay View's balcony, which was cooler than the inside of the bar. However, the noise of Magsaysay Drive was loud and constant. The continual honking of jeepney horns and the street busy with pedestrians and hawkers provided a relentless background noise which was drowned out only when the jukebox was playing.

I sat down holding Marilyn's hand as if it might be for the last time. I started buying girlie drinks for her to pay for her time. I would steal an occasional kiss and cuddle, and savored her being next to me. She smelled so good from the soap, shampoo and perfume that she used. She was extremely pretty and shapely. Her jet black hair and the sparkle that was always in her eyes were enchanting. She was so feminine! I was truly in love. I felt that I had finally emerged from the several unsuccessful attempts at relationships with girls in high school and in my earlier days in the Marines. I was in a euphoric mood and mesmerized by her presence. I knew that it was going to be hard being away from her for the next few weeks as we went in-country.

Then a group of three men dressed in civilian clothes came in from the staircase. This was highly unusual since we all had to be in uniform in town. They seemed a little older than us. They looked around, seeing that the place was packed and there were not too many seats left. They walked over to our table overlooking the street and asked if they could join us since the other tables on the floor did not have enough space to accommodate the three of them. I agreed to them sitting with us, not thinking that it could do any harm.

We soon began talking and I learned that they were involved in some sort of photo intelligence and were US Navy enlisted men. The older man sitting next to me seemed as if he was the head honcho and liked to chat. At times he made me uneasy because he kept putting his hand on my knee. He sensed the uneasiness that I was feeling and explained that he had had a lot of years in the Philippines and was used to the local style of talking and that it was not unusual for a man to be touching another man; this was not a sign of homosexuality. His explanation only partially relieved my anxiety. The other two men were talking to each other and ignoring everything else. I was holding on to Marilyn thinking that this was not how I wished to spend the last night with her. Suddenly one of the other two got up, walked around to stand in front of Marilyn, looked at me and said, "Can I dance with your girlfriend, marine?" Trusting Marilyn and being on my own turf, I felt okay about it and said, "Sure," throwing in a smile. Also, it was now after 9:00 pm and all of us were going to have to be back on the ship soon. As an enlisted man I had to be physically on the ship when liberty ended at 2300 hours. Since this was a group of enlisted men I figured they would have the same curfew for their liberty.

The two of them went to the dance floor and started to dance and chat. By now I was getting a little apprehensive with one man touching my knee and the squid on the dance floor chatting to my lady. After two or three dances he went down the staircase and Marilyn went to the toilet. A few minutes later when Marilyn emerged she gave me a little smile and went down the stairs to the ground floor bar. This did not seem right. I told the other two that I had to get back aboard, shook hands and rushed downstairs to see where Marilyn was. When I got to the ground floor I saw Mama Rosita and asked her where Marilyn had gone. She told me the sailor had paid the bar fine and the two of them had left. I suddenly felt as if the sky had fallen in. Seeing the hurt in my eyes Mama Rosita told me not to worry as there were many other women in the world, etc. It was not what I wished to hear at that moment. Anyway, the mamasan may as well not have been there at all. I gave a polite smile and went out to get on a jeepney for the main gate. Right away I found a main gate jeepney with a space and quickly took my seat. Inside I felt as if my heart was going to stop! I had been hurt before by a woman but nothing like this. I had been betrayed by the person that I loved the most in the world. I wanted to cry, shout and scream, all at once. I was overwhelmed with grief.

I got aboard the *Princeton* and went to the sleep area I had been allocated by the onboard radio relay technicians. I did not change or shower. I just took off my shoes and lay down in my uniform and tried to cry. I could not cry, I felt so much grief. I was awake all night.

Morning did not bring any relief from the pain. The lack of sleep from the night before simply magnified the intensity of it. I finally mustered enough energy to get a shower, change to my utilities and take my place in the chow line for breakfast. After the long wait in line I was served breakfast. I then realized that I was not hungry and ended up throwing the entire meal away.

I hated Marilyn but then I loved her; my emotions were very confused. In my mind this was far worse than stopping a bullet. I rationalized the situation by saying to myself that it was an economic decision for her and what could I expect from a whore from a bar? The pain was nearly unbearable. The situation was made worse because we were now going into shipboard life and shipboard life gave a marine a lot of free time. I had a bad case of heartbreak and did not need free time to ponder over what had happened. I would have major moments of depression followed by feelings of anxiety. I was irritated and avoided even fellow marines who were my friends.

I found a good position on the catwalk under the flight deck to watch the preparations for getting underway. Before noon the

Princeton was steaming out of Subic Bay for the open sea. The breeze created by the ship's movement felt good on my face but I was haunted by the scene of Marilyn's betrayal. Over and over again I thought of what had happened and could not come to any rational conclusion.

The next three days and nights were difficult since I was in shock from the last day at the Bay View and not getting much sleep. On the fourth day at sea we were already off the coast of Vietnam. That night I sat on the flight deck as we cruised along the shoreline. What seemed like a fireworks display was taking place onshore, with flashes and tracer rounds reaching into the air. I was wondering what it would be like to be ashore where the fireworks were taking place. Watching this from the flight deck was like a dream. I'm sure that it was a nightmare for those that were in the middle of the fight.

Around 14 June we pulled into Cam Ranh Bay. This bay, an inlet of the South China Sea, is in Khánh Hòa Province on the southeastern coast of Vietnam, just south of Nha Trang and approximately 290 clicks (kilometers) northeast of Saigon. Cam Ranh Bay is considered the finest deepwater shelter in Southeast Asia and as we steamed into its middle we could see why. It had the whitest sand I've ever seen. From the blue color of the water it was evident that it was very deep.

We did not drop anchor but the *Princeton* came to a near stop and a helicopter flew off the flight deck with a shore party to collect our mail. Mail was our lifeline to the world back home and we longingly looked forward to mail calls. Because of being on a ship that was constantly on the move, a mail call was not a daily occurrence. Both sailors and marines looked in eager anticipation at the helicopter as it took off, landed on a dock and then returned with several large mail bags. After the shore party arrived back, we steamed out of Cam Ranh Bay.

Two days later, on the morning of 16 June, we had a mail call for communications platoon, Headquarters and Supply Company. I received a letter from my sister Sandy. Hearing from her made me homesick and it only deepened the depression I was experiencing.

CHAPTER TWENTY-FOUR

DECKHOUSE 1

I remember the start of Operation Deckhouse 1 extremely well since it began on my twenty-second birthday (18 June 1966). We were up before dawn and had our traditional pre-combat operation breakfast of steak and eggs. The logistics of a vertical amphibious assault are mind-boggling. The *Princeton* was like a beehive with Sea Horse choppers coming and going between the ship and the landing zones (LZ) on shore. As we were waiting our turn for the choppers from the flight deck of the *Princeton*, the first casualty was on the way back; a young marine had a hand grenade go off in the pocket of his utilities pants, which blew his leg off. Since this was our first casualty, it caused much interest on the *Princeton*. Marines from the other two ships in the special landing force went ashore on landing craft.

On deck, as a group of choppers was returning, we saw one of the Sea Horses hit the water and everyone was amazed that it did not float! It was on the surface for only a few seconds. It went under like a stone.

As I was about to board my designated chopper to be ferried to my LZ my shop chief from the communications company looked at me and said, "Be careful!" The shop chief had given me to the wire section and I was to work with a Sergeant Dorsey (I think this was the spelling) as a wireman. I felt this was hypocritical of him, since he had no need to send me into combat. I was the only telephone/teletype technical in the battalion and the two radio technicians were to stay aboard the ship. However, deep inside I was a marine and I wanted to go in-country. I would function as a wireman under Sergeant Dorsey, whom I respected as a fair man and a good marine. The other technician who was going ashore with the command post (CP) was the ground radar technician who was attached to S2 (intelligence). He was used as a scout on several occasions since ground radar in those days was very bulky and we never used it on combat operations.

There was an exciting feeling as the chopper was about to depart. Since the chopper was not fitted with seats, which made it quicker to board and get out, we sat on the deck in the cabin. Flying towards our LZ we could see the shoreline as we passed over the beach heading inland. I remembered the words of our gunny not to load our rifles. However, on the way in, as I was sitting without a magazine in my rifle, the chopper's door gunner took one of the magazines from my utility belt, inserted it into my M14, and locked and loaded it for me. He then looked at me and gave me the thumbs up sign. He had been back and forth a few times and did not know if we were going into a hot LZ or not.

The LZ was at the bottom of a hill in Song Cau, somewhere north of Cameron Bay. We all left the helicopter as quickly as possible and then the chopper left the LZ. We started to hump (hike) up the small hill to a flat area where we were to set up our CP. As we were moving up the hill, I became aware of how beautiful and peaceful the Vietnam countryside was. It was not what I had expected after seeing so many war movies.

We arrived at a flat point and started to establish the CP. Being the biggest (6 ft 4 in), I carried the battalion switchboard (an SB22). To make sure that the CP could communicate with various areas around the perimeter, the wireman and I started on the laborious task of setting up communications to the battalion's perimeter by using phones (EE8s) and our SB22 switchboard. We needed to dig a hole in the middle of the CP to house the switchboard, and fighting holes around the perimeter. There was a steep part of the hill at the back of the CP and it would have been difficult for the Vietcong (VC) to launch an attack from there.

When we started to dig fighting holes, I worked on one with several members of the Comms platoon and remember asking one of the sergeants whether we would be digging more fighting holes as a second line of defense that we could retreat back into. He said, "What second line of defense? This is it." An older sergeant, who had had experience in Korea, came by at that point and asked, "Are you sure that you don't want to dig deeper holes around the perimeter?" We told him we thought they were deep enough. He went away laughing and saying, "We will see tomorrow." Most of us were not convinced that the holes needed to be deeper so they stayed the same depth.

As we were settling in, there was a sound similar to several bees buzzing through the CP and all the old-timers hit the deck. I, along with most others, soon realized that this was rifle fire and the sound was made by bullets. In-country you learn very quickly, and we all hit the deck. This was the start of the harassment that would continue throughout Deckhouse 1.

One of the Comms platoon members, whom we called Blue, drew perimeter duty and was to man one of our new fighting holes with another Comms platoon marine. Each fighting hole on the perimeter was manned by two marines. Watches were normally in shifts of four on and four off, shared between the two men in the fighting hole. When attacked, everyone in the fighting holes fights.

Blue (I cannot remember his real name, but he was a great young marine) was a little younger than me. He always told the story of how he wanted to win the Congressional Medal of Honor and join the US Army Special Forces. He thought that to be able to wear the Green Beret was the coolest thing on Earth. He wanted to be in a position where he never had to endure another inspection and everyone had to salute him; only winners of the Medal of Honor had such a privilege.

Darkness approached and since I had not drawn perimeter duty I was to stay in the center of the CP. The gunny had made sure that those of us in the center were not "locked and loaded" (that is, we did not have a round in the chamber ready to shoot, once the safety-catch was off). Our magazines were of fifteen rounds; a magazine holds twenty, but we never fully loaded, to prevent the spring from wearing out too quickly. Those of us in the center of the CP paired up and put our ponchos together to give us shelter for the night.

The action started early; volleys of fire started running through the CP. The VC's rifles had a distinctively different sound from our M14s. The first volley of fire from the VC caused me to lock and load inside my poncho tent. One of the senior sergeants over by the switchboard instantly yelled, "Unchamber that fucking round!" In my mind I was thinking, "Aw shit, Clubb fucked up again." Luckily for me it was so dark that they did not know who had loaded the chamber of his rifle. It was the job of the marines on the perimeter to do the shooting. It was a helpless feeling to hear the rounds whistle through the

CP and not be able to return the fire. But of course if someone inside the perimeter were to fire, the round could cause a friendly-fire casualty.

None of us got much sleep that night since we were on edge. The dawn brought a new dry summer's day. It was amazing that in the early morning before sunrise, there was a chill in the air. The morning sun had a warm feeling and took away the veil of night that had hidden those who were harassing our perimeter.

We had our morning C-ration (the C-rations were from the 1940s) and, as normal, everyone tried to get the B-ration, which had the fruit cocktail. Ham and lima beans were always left for the late comers. Not many marines liked the layer of fat that covered the ham and lima beans. Each C-ration contained a package that had cigarettes, matches, a Sterno tablet to warm the main course of the meal, toilet paper and eating utensils. The cigarettes were Lucky Strikes, but with a green logo instead of the red one that we were used to seeing in the mid-1960s. I understand that the logo was green up to the end of WWII. Being a non-smoker, I would trade my cigarettes either for food or for additional toilet paper. We would take our P38 (C-ration can-opener) and make ourselves a little stove out of the C-ration can that normally contained the bread. We did this by cutting a series of holes on the side of the can near the unopened end after we'd taken the bread out. (The bread's taste brought back memories of the smell of formaldehyde in my high school biology class.) We would put the Sterno tablet from the package into the bottom of the modified can and light it. We would open and warm the can containing the main course from the C-ration on the self-made stove. It always amazed us that the C-rations had been manufactured in the 1940s and here we were consuming them in 1966.

While eating morning chow I could see Blue digging the fighting hole deeper. The prediction of the senior sergeant was correct; after the previous night's attack by the VC, Blue realized that the hole was much too shallow. Blue was adding an amazing amount of depth to the hole. The volleys of fire in the night from the VC had convinced him that this was necessary. Later in the morning, choppers from the *Princeton* brought in fresh provisions. We settled into a routine of C-ration meals and being the CP for the line companies doing their search and destroy sweeps.

The next evening I was assigned to the perimeter with one of my fellow Comms platoon marines. As I sat my first watch I was amazed to see fires on the hillsides. They must have been lit by VC forces! Foley and I manned the fighting hole that Blue had dug deeper. Early in the evening the VC hit again. This time the fire fight lasted for about thirty minutes. The report of their rifles would be heard and then be answered by our M14s. Meanwhile, the "metal bees" were screaming through the CP. We were told not to worry about the bullets that we could hear because you wouldn't hear the one that hit you. However, we were hearing a lot! My fighting-hole mate said, "It's not supposed to be like this," and let out a slightly nervous laugh. This was contagious. I went into a fit of laughter and the two of us started rolling around uncontrollably. The VC must have wondered what kind of crazy men they were engaging in combat with. We soon regained our composure as one of our Comms platoon mates, who was running ammo, stopped to see if we needed resupplying and to see what we found so funny. We had the advantage on the VC since we were dug in on the hillside and had the high ground. I guess they knew we were the CP because of all the chopper activity in the day.

During the evening, with the four hours on and four hours off, it was hard not to get "dog-tired" fatigued. The stillness of the night coupled with fatigue is very sleep-inducing but no marine wants to fall asleep at his post. In the US Marines Corps I learned early how fatigued it is possible to get. In the Infantry Training Regiment we were allowed to sleep very little for the full twenty-eight-day duration of the ITR course. Also, I remember, later on, walking a post on guard duty at Camp Pendleton and, as had happened in my first posting after telephone and teletype repair school, seeing a light about 100 meters away, blinking my eyes and then finding myself standing under the light. I had walked 100 meters asleep! Again, the early morning brought a chill in the air as the dew fell. Dawn was always great to see.

The next day we had a Huey helicopter flying around, broadcasting announcements in Vietnamese over speakers. I think this may have been the work of the Army PsyOps

(Psychological Operations) Group. We were told that they were advising the locals about a curfew at 1800 hours. They were urging the VC to surrender. In the area of the CP we found lots of leaflets written in Vietnamese as well as pictures showing how to surrender. The US Army made much use of the PsyOps Group to deal with the VC. They must have dropped thousands of leaflets.

It soon became a routine of being hit in the night and sleeping what little we could during the day. Daytime sleep was greatly disturbed by the time spent fighting the flies that tried to land on your face. Later in the operation, a ship with large guns moved in offshore and our line companies started to get naval gun-fire support from onboard. I remember a tree in front of the CP perimeter going up in a cloud of smoke. It was set on fire by our air/naval gun-fire team and the naval gunners on the ship sighting in.

A ground radar technician friend of mine with the S2 section went out with our S2 officer, to check a village after it had been hit by naval gun-fire. The guns had been called in after one of our line companies reported being fired on from within the village. The destruction that he described was massive. He said the houses were reduced to rubble and that he had seen a woman who was still alive sitting with her intestines hanging out. It seemed like an unequal exchange: sniper fire from the village and naval gun-fire in return. I don't know what size the shells were but they sounded like freight trains when they went over us. He convinced me that I would never want to be on the receiving end of naval gun-fire.

Our men had found a diagram in the village of our CP with all the fighting holes marked. During their attacks the VC would try to get us to return fire so that they could see the layout of the CP (a procedure called reconnaissance by fire).

Again, we had problems with hand grenades. (As already mentioned, our first casualty had been caused by one of our troop's own hand grenade.) In the Comms platoon, we were instructed to wrap all of our grenades with black communication tape to keep the spoon on in case the pin came out accidentally. This added an additional step when using the grenade. You had first to remove the tape from the grenade before pulling the pin and then throwing it. Also, the South Vietnamese troops who had joined us as interrogators were accumulating the grenades. The gunny made us retrieve them from these troops since he was afraid that they would throw one inside the CP perimeter during a fire fight. (Visions of me chambering a round during a fire fight came back.) One very quiet night I was on watch with my fighting-hole mate asleep in the hole. I was trying to stay awake when my attention was drawn by the distinctive ping of a spoon coming off a grenade. I heard the grenade land very close to our hole. I woke up my fighting-hole mate in getting myself as deep into the hole as possible. The blast sent dirt raining into the hole. After the explosion, we looked around and saw that an ammo can at the back of the ledge of the hole was peppered with shrapnel. I realized that it could have been my face if I had not been alert. I owe my thanks and probably my life to Blue for a job well done in digging the hole so deep. We did not know where the grenade had come from. It was not a usual VC grenade and by the sound of the spoon coming off, I know that it must have been one of ours. Perhaps it was from another hole, or from the South Vietnamese troops with us, or perhaps a VC had picked one up that a fellow marine had thrown, undone the tape and returned it. It did not matter, we were spared injury.

As the operation progressed we accumulated prisoners from the line companies whom the South Vietnamese troops interrogated in the CP. The army did their own interrogations, but in the Marine Corp South Vietnamese troops were used. After interrogation, the prisoners were taken by chopper to I do not know where. Most of the young males had already fled their villages when we landed, so the majority of those caught were women, children and old men.

The interrogators had a technique of using split bamboo with which to beat the prisoners. The splits would open on impact and pinch the skin pulling off small chunks of flesh. From a short distance I observed a South Vietnamese interrogate a middle-aged man. He was first very friendly and offered the prisoner a cigarette as he smoked. He chatted to him as if he was a lifetime friend. Then the interrogator got very angry and drew his .45 pistol and threatened the man. When this did not bring satisfaction he used the pistol to hit the man on the side of the head. This caused him to bleed from the mouth. He pushed the man from his squatting position to the ground and started kicking him. I moved away not wishing to see any more.

To deal with the nightly harassment from attacks, one great plan was to set up trip flares in front of the perimeter. The flare was tied to a small tree and a trip line was set. In theory, a VC would come up to the perimeter and trip the flare, enabling us to see him and take him out. That evening, for some reason, several grenades were tossed over the hill in front of the CP's perimeter. One of them on explosion cut the line on a trip flare causing it to light. We looked nervously in vain for the VC who had set off the flare. Soon the flare set fire to the bush and we were fighting a small mountain blaze in front of the perimeter. If there were any VC around they must have wondered what on earth we were doing!

Another "great idea" was to set up an ambush and catch the VC before they got to our lines. Turtle and I were on the perimeter at the spot where the ambush party was to return. The word was, not to fire until the ambush party was inside the perimeter again. Darkness set in and the ambush party went out through the perimeter, next to the fighting hole where Turtle and I were hunkered down. It was quiet for over an hour, then we heard a fire-fight break out in front of our hole, and about five minutes later the ambush party rushed back inside the perimeter. One of the marines in the ambush party had sneezed as the ambush was about to be sprung and the VC had started to fire on the party before rushing off. The next day our patrol found blood so the ambush party had hit one or more of the VC before they ran.

One evening, the ship providing naval gun-fire started to shoot illumination rounds that would light up the night almost as bright as daylight. While on my watch, an illumination round went off and I saw what I thought was a person standing very still some 200 yards down the hill. I woke my fighting-hole partner and pointed to what I'd seen; he agreed it looked like a person. I remember my breath deepening and hearing my heart beating. I checked to make sure that I had my battle sights and taking careful aim I squeezed off two rounds. Another illumination round went off and the target was gone.

The next day, an army chopper landed in our CP and out steps a general looking for our commanding officer. He gave me a snappy salute, I nodded back. This made me a minor hero to my Comms platoon members. One of them said, "Only Thumper would not return a salute to a general!" I pointed out that in the field we never salute!

CHAPTER TWENTY-FIVE

OPERATION NATHAN HALE

ON 28 June 1966, Operation Deckhouse 1 came to an end and we started a joint operation with the US Army called Nathan Hale. Our command post was taken by helicopter to a local village that was the HQ of an army unit of the 101 Airborne. It was a semi-permanent camp that was well established. We had not returned to the *Princeton* so we were still very fatigued from Deckhouse 1.

The village was made up of a number of families belonging to South Vietnamese soldiers. Life was far better here than the CP had experienced during Operation Deckhouse 1. We still had our C-rations, but the army had a field kitchen and a mess tent set up. We challenged some of the soldiers to a volleyball game on a court that they had created next to the mess tent. If we won they would let us have their hot meal. We won and they honored the agreement; it was a great feeling to eat freshly-cooked food.

The village had a well and, using some communications wire as a rope and our helmets as buckets, we got water to bathe with. We tied the wire to the straps of the helmet, then lowered the helmet into the well to reach the water, which was about two meters down. We would pour the water over ourselves and soap down, and then collect another helmet of water and rinse off the soap. Some of the village women seemed amused with the new additions to the village and came to help pour the water over us as we washed. We wore different field uniforms and were a lot dirtier than the army troops in the village, so we must have caused some curiosity. It was a great feeling to get clean. However, our utilities were still dirty from the ten days of Deckhouse 1 and we had to put them on over our freshly washed bodies.

Some of the South Vietnamese soldiers who were friends with each other would hold hands as they walked down the street of the village. This drew any number of catcalls from some of us marines who did not understand this behaviour and found it hard to deal with. I guess that we were just not briefed enough on the local culture. Perhaps the catcalls would have happened anyway as we were getting an impression that we were the ones doing most of the fighting and the South Vietnamese troops were only eager to interrogate. Perhaps this was an unfair assessment since we had only been in-country for a few days.

The second day, my radar technician friend from S2 came and told me of a prisoner who was being kept in a pig pen close by. He had been taken by the army troops the night before. He must have learned of the prisoner from a briefing with the battalion S2 officer. Out of curiosity, the two of us went over to see him. We arrived to find a person of tiny stature with his hands tied behind his back sitting in pig shit and mud. I do not know what I was expecting but he sure was an unfortunate young man. He was only wearing his skivvies. He looked very thin and frail, but I knew that he would kill me in an instant if given the chance. The old AK-47, or any other weapon the Vietcong used, was a great leveler and a tiny person can bring down the biggest of men. He looked like a boy of not more than fifteen years of age. It was hard to tell, since we could not accurately judge the age of the Vietnamese. His face was badly battered from his interrogation. It looked as if he had a broken nose and he had a lot of dried blood around his mouth and nostrils. There were slash wounds on his body, possibly from interrogation. I remember he looked me in the eye with a look that was full of hate. I understand that this prisoner had already been interrogated by a US Army intelligence officer and possibly also by the South Vietnamese troops. Even seeing the hate he had for me, I felt a little sorry for him since his chances of living were not great, now that he was in the hands of the South Vietnamese Army. On Deckhouse 1, I saw the methods the South Vietnamese soldiers used with suspected VC. The many years of war had made the Vietnamese a very hard group of people.

We had a quiet time of it during our stay in this village on Operation Nathan Hale, as the perimeter was the responsibility of the army. I know that our line companies were on a search-and-destroy mission supporting the army, so we in the CP were not as busy as when the special landing force was on its own. It was as if we were guests and we had a good life here for a few days. This was quite a change from the constant harassment by the VC while on Deckhouse 1.

All things must come to an end and Nathan Hale was soon over, without me ever hearing a single shot fired in anger during the operation. On 1 July 1966, we were taken by chopper back to the *Princeton* and sailed for Subic Bay.

CHAPTER TWENTY-SIX

BACK TO SUBIC BAY AND OLONGAPO

WE arrived back in Subic Bay on 5 July 1966. As we were entering port I learned that I had been assigned shore patrol duty for that evening. We were lucky that we were able to dock at the main aircraft carrier dock close to the Spanish Gate restaurant. This was good since we did not have to rely on the liberty boats.

I really wanted to see Marilyn even though she had betrayed me. Doing shore patrol was like divine intervention saving me from going back to the Bay View bar. I was still in love with her but tried hard to keep her from my mind. In-country it was easier, since it was like being in another world. I got into my khaki uniform and reported to the officer of the day with the other marines and squids who were to pull (do) shore patrol for the evening. We were led off ship to a local Military Police (MP) station for our briefing along with men from other ships. Some squids had been through the routine before and we were divided into groups of experienced and non-experienced servicemen. The experienced group picked out who would walk shore patrol together. Olongapo was divided on racial lines. The main street was for white bars and there was a street that went off to the side forming a fork and that was where the black bars were located. The first experienced shore patrol group was made up of two white squids who had to walk the black area. The shore patrol teams were two per patrol for the white area and three per patrol for the black area. The two squids who had drawn the black part of Olongapo looked over and pointed at me and said, "We want him." One of the squids was a petty officer second class, making him equivalent to a sergeant. Since he had done this before I was confident that it would be okay. That was the first time in my life I had been picked as first choice for anything. Being 6 feet 4 inches tall and now filled out from my four years in the Marines I guess I did have a presence.

It is better to be on the drinking side of Olongapo than to be on shore patrol. When you're sober, things are not the same. We would walk into the bars to check that things were in order. I met Sergeant Dorsey, who was great, greeting me as his long-lost brother. I also met several other black communication platoon marines and things were reasonably peaceful.

Later in the evening, as we were walking down the street, an MP paddy wagon showed up and the MPs disappeared into a bar. They came out with another shore patrol group and a black squid protesting all the way. I heard the black squid say, "You fucking chucks cannot let a man walk out in dignity." They then took him to the paddy wagon and attempted to put him in the back. We did not join in since there were already five people trying to get this one miscreant into the vehicle. The black squid was objecting to being physically pushed in and was trying hard to stay out. We were summoned by the MPs to help. As we joined in I saw a crowd developing and heard verbal protests from the crowd over the treatment of the squid. It did not help that we were all white. I said, "Let the man get in himself." Everyone stopped for a moment and looked at each other. He looked at me and the MPs. We let him go and he climbed in the back of the wagon. He looked at me and said, "Thanks, man."

The three of us had a big adrenalin rush from the incident. We went into the bar that the black squid had been dragged out from, and as we got around to the back of it, the Philippine bartender set up three shots of whiskey. We were not supposed to drink, but the senior squid accepted the drinks and we each took a shot. We learned that the black squid had hit one of the bar girls and smashed her head up against the wall, injuring her very badly.

When the evening ended, I made my way back to the *Princeton,* went straight to the air conditioned radio room and fell asleep very quickly. When I woke the following morning I walked out onto the bridge and saw that a service was being held on the flight deck. I had not heard that it was taking place, as I had gone straight to the radio relay room the previous night. I put on the khaki uniform that I had worn for the previous evening's shore patrol and went down through the hanger deck, back up to the flight deck and got behind where Comms platoon was formed. When the service was over I walked over to the Comms platoon from behind and got into the last squad formation. Our platoon sergeant started roll call and luckily I got marked as in the formation since if you missed the formation you lost several days of liberty. The service was for the five Marines who were killed in action on Deckhouse I and Operation Nathan Hale. The handout from the service read:

MEMORIAL SERVICE FOR

Marines of Battalion Landing Team 3/5 who died in the service of their country on operations Deck House 1 and Nathan Hale in the Republic of Vietnam 18 June through July 2, 1966.

****

PFC Louis Xavier CABRERA, Jr.	18 June 1966
Blue Island, Illinois	
PFC Terry Wayne BUCKLER	18 June 1966
Fenton, Michigan	
Corporal Charles Herman HILL	18 June 1966
Forreston, Illinois	
Corporal Ernest Eustance PEREZ	30 June 1966
Lone Pine, California	
Lance Corporal Willie L. COLLIER	24 June 1966
Oceanside, California	

****

O God, rest the souls of Thy servants with the saints, where there is no sickness, nor sadness, nor sighing, but life without ending.

Byzantine Liturgy

I do love my country's good with a respect more tender, more Holy and profound than mine own life.

Shakespeare

It was ironic that three of the five marines who had died had been killed on my twenty-second birthday. I realized that war takes the young. There was no one on the list of those who died in these two operations above the rank of corporal. They were all in their late teens or very early twenties.

Most of my fellow Comms platoon shipmates went ashore for liberty. I was reluctant to do so since I was still thinking about Marilyn and felt that I should not see her. I finished noon chow and went back to the radio relay room and settled into the book *Catch 22*. I could not concentrate on my reading and at about 4:00 pm I dressed in my khaki uniform and made my way into Olongapo for liberty.

As I arrived in front of the Bay View bar I signaled the jeepney driver that I wanted to get off. I paid him the fifty centavos fee, got off and stood in front of the entrance. I was reluctant to go in and was about to go to another bar when suddenly one of the girls who knew me came up. She looked as if she had seen a ghost and said in her Philippine inflexion, "Hi, Lee! Wow, last night Marilyn asked your friends what had happened to you and they said you were killed. I'm so glad to see you!" She took me by the hand and led me into the bar. We went up the stairs where the dance floor was full. I saw Marilyn dancing with a squid. Her friend shouted to Marilyn in Tagalog, "Sis, hanahanap ka nito!" She turned and saw me and, looking very shocked, screamed, "Lee!" She ran over to me and jumped up with her hands around my neck, wrapping her legs around my hips and hugging me tight. Her eyes suddenly filled with tears and she said, "I thought you were dead." She started kissing me and I did not know what to do. I tried to get her to stand but she kept hugging me and I had the weight of her body on me which felt so good. I had thought that I would go in and say goodbye to her for betraying me. All of the pain of the past few weeks suddenly went away. I paid the bar fine and we went to the hotel next door where we stayed till I had to report back to the ship.

Back on ship the next morning and on the way to morning chow, I met two of my corporal shipmates whom I had introduced to the Bay View. They were having a good laugh about the joke they had played on Marilyn. I told them that it was a "fucking bad joke." One said, "Things are okay now. Remember, she fucked that squid and betrayed you on your last night before we went in-country; a little payback does no harm." I said, "I know. I guess I'm just horny." He replied saying, "There are thousands of whores in Olongapo and you only chase one!" Then adding, "Did you have a good fuck?" I replied, "It's none of your fucking business!" As we were walking they went on laughing, one telling me, "You should never get so attached to an Olongapo whore; remember the round-eyed pussy in the land of the big PX!" I shouted back "Fuck you." He rebutted, "If you fuck me you'll never go back to women. I'm so good!" We all laughed and went off to chow together.

We learned that we were all to be given ninety-six-hour liberty passes. When I was given my pass the next day, I found Marilyn and told her that I wished to see something of Manila. She suggested staying at the Aloha Hotel, which was at 2150 Roxas Boulevard in Malate. It was supposed to be reasonable and nicely located. She said she would take the next day off but would come to Manila, as soon as she finished that night. She gave me instructions as to where the bus terminus was and what bus I should catch for Manila. I went back to the ship and got my shower gear and a change of underwear since I would be away for two nights. I went to the bus station in Olongapo to get the bus Marilyn had told me to catch. The bus ride was quite an adventure. I was the only non-Filipino on board and it took several hours to reach the terminus in Manila. Along the way the bus would stop every once in a while for people to get out and relieve themselves on the side of the road. I fell into the pattern of urinating every time the bus stopped.

As we pulled into the terminus there was a jeepney waiting with two Filipinos sitting in it. It was painted green with the letters "USMC" on the side as if it was an official vehicle. The Filipinos saw me in my uniform and started to shout, "Hey marine, need a ride? We are cheap; let us take you to your hotel!" As I was walking toward the door, an older man on the bus behind me tapped me on my shoulder and I turned to see a family of husband, wife and teenage daughter. The man said, "Be careful with them, they are no good." I thanked him for his concern. It shows that there are good people everywhere.

I left the bus and got into the jeepney. They let me have the front seat next to the driver so I rode shotgun. I told them that I needed to get to the Aloha Hotel on Roxas Boulevard. They said that they knew where it was and asked if I wanted a tour before going to the hotel. I said, "No, maybe tomorrow when my girlfriend arrives." They took me to the hotel and charged far more than the fifty centavos I was used to paying for a jeepney ride in Olongapo. I paid them and they said that they would pick me up the next day for a tour.

I checked into the hotel and had a shower. Later I went out and tried to find some civilian clothes. I found an outdoor market but was only able to get a pair of pants that were about two inches too short and a tight shirt. I walked around and found a

Mexican restaurant called Papagayo's. I had a burrito and a beer, but the taste was not the same as in East Los Angeles. I was tired and started walking back to the hotel to wait for Marilyn.

I found the Philippines and particularly Manila an amazing place. At that time, the Philippines had the number two economy in Asia, only behind Japan. However, it had a Wild West feel about it. Their new president, Ferdinand E. Marcos, had been elected at the end of the previous year. Since I had to wait for Marilyn I bought a local newspaper, *The Manila Times*. I was impressed by the political commentary; here was a country that did not shy away from criticizing its politicians.

Being tired from the bus trip I walked directly back to the hotel and continued to read the newspaper. I then gave up and fell asleep. Marilyn arrived at the hotel around 3:00 am. She had left work early and taken a night bus for Manila. It was great to see her. I told her about the two men in the jeepney and she was not too happy about the price I had been charged for the fare. She was so tired that after she showered she fell asleep instantly. I lay next to her watching her. I had often thought of her while in-country, one minute hating her and the next dreaming of a moment like this.

The next morning we were woken up by a phone call from the two from the jeepney. They were in the hotel lobby. Marilyn got on the phone and gave them a scolding in Tagalog for ripping me off the day before. Needless to say, we did not take the tour. We went to breakfast and came back to the hotel room. We did not get to see much of Manila as we stayed in the hotel till the next morning. The following day I put on the civilian clothes that I had bought, for the ride back to Olongapo, and Marilyn said, "Honey, put your uniform back on, you're so handsome in it!" I had to admit that the civilian clothes were not very good. I changed back to my uniform and we checked out of the hotel to get the early bus back to Olongapo. Marilyn had to get back for duty that evening in the Bay View. As we sat on the bus on the ride back I was holding her hand and cuddling her. I liked the nice brown color of the skin on the back of her hand. I had not seen much of Manila but the trip provided two of the nicest days I had had up to that time.

I fell back into the pattern of spending time with Marilyn by paying her bar fine and taking her to a short-time hotel. One night we lost track of time and I saw that I had exceeded the 2300-hour deadline to be back at the ship. It was already 2315 hours when I left the hotel. I rushed back to the ship but was written up for being late by the officer of the day. The next day my liberty card was pulled. It was July 12. Our company gunny was punishing me without formally charging me, thus keeping my record clean, by restricting me to the ship. Now another group of men was on their ninety-six-hour liberty so the ship was very quiet.

On July 13 at about 11:00 am we were told that we were going to leave for Vietnam again. Little did we know that the NVA (North Vietnamese Army) 324 Division had just invaded Quang Tri Province with some 10,000 to 12,500 troops. This was the start of the Division's invasion. We did not know then what had happened to necessitate this sudden departure.

Shore patrols and MPs were sent into town to round up everyone. Unfortunately, some people had gone to Manila so we were going to have to leave without them. As the troops started to come back aboard I saw my fellow Bay View bar raider friends. They came over to me and had a small package. They told me that Marilyn had sent it to me. I opened it and found a silver crucifix. I was told that she had had a priest bless it and I was to wear it on combat operations. It nearly brought tears to my eyes. I had missed her since my liberty card had been pulled and she knew we would leave soon.

That evening we left Subic Bay and headed to float off the coast of Vietnam. While still in range, the choppers picked up some of our fellow marines who had been left behind and brought them back on board.

CHAPTER TWENTY-SEVEN

DECKHOUSE 2

EARLY in the morning of July 16, we were woken before sunrise for a steak and egg breakfast, so we knew that we were going on an operation. I guess this was because we would not have freshly-cooked food for a while as we would be eating C-rations. Sure enough, Operation Deckhouse 2 had started. I learned later that the operation area was called the "Street Without Joy." We were setting up the command post about thirteen kilometers northeast of Dong Ha in a place named Gio Lien Province.

We did not know what was happening since we were only a cog in a wheel. We could not figure out the purpose of Deckhouse 2, but it was obviously a staging area for the battalion landing team in preparation for the operation to follow, Operation Hastings. We did not know that during the late June and early July of 1966, Marine reconnaissance units operating south of the Demilitarized Zone (DMZ) had been reporting increased numbers of uniformed regular North Vietnamese Army (NVA) troops. On 6 July 1966, troops of the South Vietnamese Army (SVA or ARVN – Army of the Republic of Vietnam) 1st Division captured an NVA soldier near a landmark called the Rockpile. He identified himself as being from the 812th Regiment of the 324B NVA Division and said that the other regiments of the Division had also moved into South Vietnam. On 9 July, a lieutenant from the 812th Regiment surrendered in the same area and advised that the 324B Division's mission was to liberate Quang Tri Province.[3]

The operation started just as Deckhouse 1 had done, with marines being loaded up on the choppers and flown in-country. This time, neither my shop chief nor the radio technicians who were to stay on the ship came up to say goodbye, so I just boarded my assigned chopper to fly to the landing zone. We lifted off the flight deck to head towards the shore and I was wondering what this operation was going to be like. As the chopper cleared the ship I did not have to be told to put a

---

[3] http://en.wikipedia.org/wiki/Operation_Hastings

magazine into my M14. As the chopper crossed the shoreline, it set down close to a beach. It was a great looking beach and could have been in any resort area of the world. However, it was empty and we were the only ones there.

When all the CP personnel were ashore we got organized, and those of us in the wire section got down to the business of setting up the wire communications to the perimeter and also the battalion's switch board.

We were in an area made up of deserted dry rice paddies. We thought that this would make it easier to dig fighting holes since we could use the walls of the rice paddy to make one side of the holes. However, as we dug we found that the water table was only about two feet down. Nevertheless, we still used the walls provided by the rice paddies to construct our fighting holes.

After we got the CP set up, we found the beach too inviting to ignore and we took turns going for a swim in the ocean. The water was beautiful. It was ironic that a country of death and destruction could have such beautiful beaches. In fact, the whole country had breathtaking scenery.

The next day, while sitting in the area that I was guarding on the perimeter, I saw a frog jumping around on the edge of the rice paddy wall. The next thing I saw was a snake strike and grab the frog and disappear into the bush. I hate snakes and there seemed to be more than a few in the old paddies. Blue killed a snake and after the snake stopped moving he took off the head and put it on his dog tag chain. Our doc warned him that a snake can still bite even after it is dead. He jokingly said if he could not have enemy ears, a snake's head would have to do. The snake's head did not smell too good after a while so he had to remove it.

We started to settle into the daily routine of CP life, and I was not sure where our line companies were. Some of them had to do a traditional landing craft assault.

As soon as we were established ashore, the operation was terminated and BLT 3/5 joined Task Force Delta in an all-Marine operation to repel the 324B Division. The two operations, Deckhouse 2 and Hastings were seamless for BLT 3/5.

On 18 July, we were taken by chopper out of Deckhouse 2 to set up the CP for Operation Hastings. I remember getting aboard the chopper and sitting in the back, and the pilot trying to take off. But we were too heavy, so the door gunner signaled for one of the marines near the door to get off. When he alighted the pilot tried again and we were still too heavy, so the door gunner signaled for another marine to alight. After the second marine got off we were finally able to fly. I was thinking that we must be in a hurry, by the way we left Subic Bay, and now for the pilot to be flying by the seat of his pants like this. Also, as we moved away from the ocean, the choppers were needed to move our line companies, so they were very busy.

For Headquarters and Service Company and the CP it was a quiet couple of days on Operation Deckhouse 2.

CHAPTER TWENTY-EIGHT

OPERATION HASTINGS

ON 18 July 1966, the chopper ride was reasonably short and we were inserted into a valley at a landing zone named Dove. We set up our 3/5 command post in what was once a very nice area of villas. In peace time it would have been an ideal setting in which to camp. The countryside was beautiful. The architecture had a French influence and the area may have been occupied by the French in the colonial days. However, I have read that Captain Haupt was not happy with the CP site. It was flat and the buildings were good landmarks that would make it easy for the North Vietnamese Army to target us. This was unlike Deckhouse 1 where we had the high ground and were better able to defend the CP.

Prior to our arrival this area was either under VC or NVA control. Battalion landing Team 3/5's CP was the first of any friendly forces (South Vietnamese, Alliance (Korean, Australian) or US) to operate in the area. The US Air Force's B-52s had recently carpet-bombed this area and we could see the craters of the large bombs around our new CP zone. They were like large swimming pools and the craters were now holding water from the rain. The concussion of the bombs had compressed the ground so much that the bottoms of the craters were like concrete. I surely would not like to have been on the receiving end of this. It must have been like hell when the bombs went off.

We began the work of setting up the wire communication for the CP. This new CP site was very different from what we had seen in Song Cau, especially since there was no one living near. It was in a valley on the flat instead of on a hillside.

The second night I heard what sounded like a roll of communication wire being unrolled. It was a clicking sound. My poncho tent mate who was the S2 radar tech listened as well. We reported it to our platoon sergeant. He listened and told us to fix bayonets and check it out. We were inside the perimeter and could not just fire our rifles. We started to crawl towards the sound with our M14s with fixed bayonets. I remember hearing my own breath and feeling my heart beat wildly, wishing that I could breathe a little less noisily. I was sure that my breathing sounded like a freight train and that anyone within several yards could hear it. It seemed like a long time before we got close to the sound. As we got close to the sound and could see where it was coming from, we realized that it was a water buffalo with an improvised bell made from a coconut shell. The coconut shell was what was making the noise. We stood up startling the buffalo. It then ran through the center of the CP right over our gunny who we heard shout, "Holy shit!" This made us break into laughter.

We met one of our Comm platoon friends the next day who had been sitting on the perimeter the evening before, and he said he had seen the water buffalo wander into the CP and come by his fighting hole. We asked him why didn't shoot it. He said, "If I had shot it, gunny would have made me bury it!"

We now had a communications wire line running from the CP to the top of the tallest hill close to the CP. We had a PRC-10 radio antenna set up on the hill so that the CP could communicate with the line companies on the move. After the second day, the wire was broken and a few of us from the wire section had to walk down the wire towards the hill. We were aware that it might be an ambush. We happily found the break a few hundred yards from the perimeter of the CP and quickly repaired it.

A daily replenishing party was put together from our CP to take water and C-rations to the top of the hill for the marines guarding the antenna. I'm not sure, but I believe that the marines on the hill were Recon Marines, and in addition to guarding the antenna, they were looking for NVA troop movement. I was ordered to join the party and carried a couple of cases of rations in a back pack on one of the replenishing trips. Other marines had a can of water on a pack rack. We had a few extra marines for security. We hiked from the CP to the top of the hill. I remember the hilltop looked barren.

The next day, as I had been there before, I was told that I would lead the replenishing party and this time I hiked up the hill as the non-commissioned officer leading the party. As we were coming back to the CP, I made everyone stop and look around very carefully as we would cross a clearing and be in the open. A small group of marines on its own would have been easy meat for a larger NVA patrol.

Our line companies were progressively moving further away from the CP in a southwesterly direction and it was decided that we needed a PRC-10 radio relay point on the top of Hill 362. On 24 July 1966, BLT 3/5's India Company was sent up the hill to establish the radio relay post. India Company was able to get to the top of Hill 362 without incident. However, when the Company started down the other side of the hill to set up a defensive perimeter, they were hit by a well-executed ambush by members of the 6th regiment of the NVA 324 Division. They were greatly outnumbered but still held the hill. A Medal of Honor was won in this battle by Lance Corporal Pitman, the citation reads:

The President of the United States takes pleasure in presenting the
MEDAL OF HONOR to
SERGEANT RICHARD A. PITTMAN
UNITED STATES MARINE CORPS
for service as set forth in the following CITATION:

For conspicuous gallantry and intrepidity at the risk of his life above and beyond the call of duty as a member of First Platoon, Company I, Third Battalion, Fifth Marines during combat operations near the Demilitarized Zone, Republic of Vietnam. On July 24, 1966, while Company I was conducting an operation along the axis of a narrow jungle trail, the leading company elements suffered numerous casualties when they suddenly came under heavy fire from a well-concealed and numerically superior enemy force. Hearing the engaged Marines' calls for more firepower, Sergeant (then Lance Corporal) Pittman quickly exchanged his rifle for a machine gun and several belts of ammunition, left the relative safety of his platoon, and unhesitatingly rushed forward to aid his comrades. Taken under intense enemy small-arms fire at point blank range during his advance, he returned the fire, silencing the enemy positions. As Sergeant Pittman continued to forge forward to aid members of the leading platoon, he again came under heavy fire from two automatic weapons which he promptly destroyed. Learning that there were additional wounded Marines fifty yards further along the trail, he braved a withering hail of enemy mortar and small-arms fire to continue onward. As he reached the position where the leading Marines had fallen, he was suddenly confronted with a bold frontal attack by 30 to 40 enemy. Totally disregarding his own safety, he calmly established a position in the middle of the trail and raked the advancing enemy with devastating machine-gun-fire. His weapon rendered ineffective, he picked up a submachine gun and, together with a pistol seized from a fallen comrade, continued his lethal fire until the enemy force had withdrawn. Having exhausted his ammunition except for a grenade which he hurled at the enemy, he then rejoined his own platoon. Sergeant Pittman's daring initiative, bold fighting spirit and selfless devotion to duty inflicted many enemy casualties, disrupted the enemy attack and saved the lives of many of his wounded comrades. His personal valor at grave risk to himself reflects the highest credit upon himself, the Marine Corps and the United States Naval Service.

LYNDON B. JOHNSON[4]

On 24 July 1966, eighteen India Company marines were killed and many wounded. This was made worse by the fact that India Company had just had eight marines killed in a firefight on 22 July 1966. India Company was really hit hard and they fought with much valor and held Hill 362 against a larger number of NVA troops. The next day the NVA was gone. To develop an LZ to get the dead and wounded out, axes and chain saws were dropped by choppers. The men of India Company had to chop down sufficient trees to allow the choppers in close enough. Also, on the *Princeton* a wooden foot locker was packed with blood for transfusions for the wounded. I heard that many *Princeton* sailors donated blood for the wounded. The foot locker was dropped in by a chopper and was found by the men; the transfusions were administered by India Company's navy corpsmen to the wounded.

One amazing story from this fight was of Private First Class Bednar, who was a radioman. During the ambush, Bednar was shot and fell unconscious; cut off from his unit he was left lying in the bush. After the battle was over the NVA started bayoneting the marines whom they found, to make sure that they were dead. Lying close to Bednar was a wounded marine. This wounded marine groaned when he was bayoneted and was immediately shot. Bednar was now conscious and hearing this, he did not move or make any noise while they bayoneted him three or four times. After being bayoneted, he continued playing

---

[4] http://en.wikipedia.org/wiki/Richard_A._Pittman

dead while the NVA took his watch, cigarettes, pistol and radio. When it got dark, he crawled up the trail towards where the rest of India Company was on top of Hill 362. It was an extremely dark night so he was able to avoid the NVA passing him on the trail by playing dead or crawling off the trail. He was able to crawl all the way back to join the remains of India Company the next morning. He had crawled nearly 150 yards with a gunshot wound and three or four bayonet wounds. One of the bayonet wounds had opened up his midsection and his intestines were hanging out.

On 26 July 1966, BLT 3/5's CP was relocated. My memory is fading and I'm not sure if we moved part of the distance by chopper but I remember our having to hike a long way to our new CP area on a hillside. Our commanding officer of Headquarters and Service Company, Captain Haupt, did not like the fact that we had our 3/5 CP in an "abandoned French chateau" on hard-to-defend flat terrain. I think one reason why we moved the CP may have been that he was finally able to get his point across to higher command that it was a mistake to be where we were. He wanted to move the CP to prevent us from being attacked by the NVA on flat ground. I read that some people think he may have saved us from the kind of slaughter that 2/5's CP later endured on Operation Prairie. To overrun a battalion CP is a big victory for the enemy. Another possibility is that we moved to be in a better position for extraction back to the *Princeton*. I am not sure what was behind the decision, but we moved our CP.

When we arrived at our new CP site, I was put in charge of getting a sound-power-phone combat loop around the perimeter of the new CP so that the perimeter fighting holes could communicate with each other. A combat loop is a complete wire loop connecting all sound power phones so that if the line is cut anywhere there is still communication between the fighting holes going the other way from the break in the line. A sound power phone does not require batteries and does not have a great range. It is good for a tight perimeter combat loop where the phone can generate enough power to carry the signal around the loop from the person's voice. I duly worked with the wiremen to get the loop in place.

On, I believe, 27 July, the remains of India Company joined us in H&S Company to help with the perimeter security of the new CP. India Company really suffered badly from the battle for Hill 362. In all, 116 Purple Hearts were awarded to India Company for Operation Hastings. When they joined H&S Company, they had only sixty-eight of the approximately 180 marines who had made up India Company when they started. The rest had been killed or seriously wounded.

The evening that India Company joined us, we had probing fire on the perimeter and one of my fellow Comms platoon marines told me how rounds from an automatic weapon were fired at his hole and he had returned the fire. He said that he was sharing the fighting hole with an India Company rifleman who had scolded him for firing back as it was only probing fire and asked him to shoot only if he had a target. He said, "If a fucker shoots at me I'm going to shoot back."

I heard that we had a friendly fire incident that evening and several mortar rounds from our own mortars landed in the new CP before the problem was sorted out. I did not wake up and never heard the mortar rounds hit. It was at that stage in an operation when you are so tired that it is hard at times to wake up. I guess between the boredom on one hand and having your adrenaline drained on the other, you get to a point when you are like a zombie.

It was my turn to pull (perform) duty on the CP switchboard. While I was sitting at the switchboard a panicky emergency call came in. A couple of the young marines on the perimeter had been playing catch with a hand grenade and the pin came out. A sergeant close by threw a helmet over the grenade to try and shield everyone, but to no avail. It went off and killed the two young marines and the sergeant. I made a patch-through call so that a medevac helicopter could retrieve them. It seemed that once again we were being killed by our own hand grenades. I wondered how this could be since the pins were so tight. If you did a "John Wayne" and pulled the pin with your teeth you would pull out your teeth instead of the pin. The pin must have been loosened to make it easier to pull.

On 29 July 1966, we broke up and moved the CP again. This time we hiked to a new location next to a very high formation of rocks called the Rockpile. It seemed like a long hike, carrying all the communications equipment from the CP, and I remember at one point while toiling up a steep hill seeing Captain Chalmers carrying something large and heavy. I turned to him and said, "Can I help you carry that, sir?" He didn't seem too pleased that I had asked and he continued to carry the heavy equipment without replying.

It seemed to me that it would be impossible to break up and move a CP on foot, and not have the enemy know. We arrived and set up our new CP site in view of the Rockpile. It was an amazing, very tall and slender rock formation. I understand that a unit of Recon Marines was stationed on top of the Rockpile all through Operation Hastings. It is now a landmark, one that a lot of former marines who visit Vietnam make a point of seeing.

On 30 July 1966, we broke up the CP and then we were conveyed to LZ Blue Jay. I remember trying to get the communications wire from our perimeter telephone lines that we had laid down. We were burning it so that the NVA could not use it. I was working as fast as I could to burn it all when I saw the chopper coming in for us. The door gunner was signaling for me to get on the chopper. I climbed on board and told Sergeant Dorsey, who was already there, that I'd been unable to get all the wire. He told me not worry about it. Our chopper lifted us out and we flew toward the coast and the *Princeton*. As we landed on the deck, the squids were lined up to give us a round of applause as we alighted from the chopper in our gear. There were a lot of camera flash bulbs going off. It seems that they knew more about the operation than we did. We were celebrities, since we had received wide coverage in the press.

By 1530 hours on 30 July 1966, all units of BLT 3/5 were aboard assigned shipping. Operation Hastings officially ended for BLT 3/5 on 30 July 1966.

Operation Hastings was a purely US Marine Corps operation with assistance from some South Vietnamese units. It seems that the Marines had inherited the area around the DMZ. There were to be other battles between the Marines and NVA 324 after Hastings. On this encounter, 183 marines were killed in action. However, we had made the NVA pay very dearly for the loss of these marine brothers; 882 of the enemy had been killed. The objectives of Operation Hastings had been met and NVA 324 was pushed back across the DMZ.

I'm reminded of the altered version, current at the time, of the 3rd verse of the 23 Psalm. It went:
Yea though I walk through the valley of the shadow of death;
I fear no evil;
since I'm the meanest mother fucker in the valley.

The men of the 324 NVA Division were certainly mean, but we were definitely the meaner on this encounter. They were far different from the VC we had come across in Song Cau on Deckhouse 1. On Deckhouse 1, the VC had located our CP and hit it repeatedly but did not engage our line companies very much. On Operation Hastings, the NVA slugged it out toe-to-toe with our line companies and proved to be well-disciplined troops who were not afraid to fight.

As a result of the actions seen, while designated BLT 3/5, we adopted the battalion slogan "Get Some!" This was to let everyone know that we wished to get some killing done and we were ready to fight.

Later, 3/5's battalion emblem was altered to add Vietnam. Until then, the battalion emblem had only Belleau Wood from the battle in France during WWI. However, we did not wear the battalion emblem patch on our uniforms, as the US Army did, even though we had one. We were told that a marine is a marine first and foremost, and we were not allowed to wear anything that would distinguish us from each other.

With the action we had seen as the special landing force BLT 3/5 during our time as part of the 3rd Marine Amphibious Force, we had now added to the history and pride of the Corps and, in particular, of 3rd Battalion/5th Marines.

Having taken part in this, our BLT duty had come to an end.

CHAPTER TWENTY-NINE

DEACTIVATION OF BLT 3/5 AND OPERATION COLORADO

WE sailed to Chu Lai and offloaded from the *Princeton* on 2 August 1966. We were moved to a temporary campsite within the Chu Lai defense perimeter. The 1st Marine Division had established its Division Headquarters in Chu Lai in March 1966, moving it from Camp Pendleton to Vietnam. Operational control of 3/5 went from the Commanding General, 3rd Marine Amphibious Force, and was reinstated with the Commanding General of 1st Marine Division. This was the official deactivation of Battalion Landing Team 3/5 and all the attached units also returned to their parent organizations. BLT 3/5 was to rejoin the 5th Marine regiment, which was part of the 1st Marine division, and was classified as in a C2 personnel category. This meant that we were not up to combat readiness, due to combat losses during Operation Hastings. Basically, we did not have enough men to be a full strength battalion. We were now to rebuild 3/5 as a functioning battalion in the 1st Marine Division.

The next day, 3 August 1966, after being offloaded, we were visited at our new encampment by Commanding General, 3rd Marine Amphibious Force, Lieutenant General Lewis W. Walt; and while speaking to all hands, he praised and congratulated us for the performance of BLT 3/5 during Operation Hastings.

We learned that the 120-day involuntary extensions to all enlistments would be cancelled as of October. This meant that I would not have to serve the full extension. Also, to encourage us to enlist, there was an order that all corporals with enough time in grade were to be promoted to sergeant E-5 effective 1 September 1966. However, 3/5 in their wisdom promoted only those who had over a year of service left or would re-enlist. The majority of us who had served the last few months with BLT 3/5 decided that we were not going to re-enlist and we were held back as corporals. It caused some hard feelings since some very junior corporals were promoted over us.

Life at Chu Lai was boring after the life on a ship as a BLT. We were in temporary tents. When it rained, a stream of water would run through the tent that I was assigned to and I would have to move my sea bag and place it on my folding bunk to keep it from getting wet. It was very different from what I had seen of the US Army's 101st Airborne Division, with which we had spent time on Operation Nathan Hale. We did have a mess tent, so we had hot chow, but it was temporary for sure.

The possibility that the Vietcong might attack and breach the defense perimeter meant we had to carry our M14 with two magazines of ten rounds each, at all times. On the second evening, someone of Native American origin got drunk and emptied his M14, randomly firing in all directions. I'm not sure what happened to him, if anything, as we did not have a brig in the temporary camp.

It did not take long before we were sent out again. Operation Colorado started for us on 6 August 1966. We loaded onto large ten-wheeled deuce and a half trucks with sandbags in the bottom of the truck bed in case the truck hit a land mine. We were sitting on a layer of sandbags. I had found the choppers of special landing force BLT 3/5 duty far more comfortable. We had all the gear and the equipment with us, to set up the battalion command post. We left Chu Lai at first light in a large convoy. We were still traveling when it became dark. Somewhere around 1900 hours, the front of the convoy was hit and all had to offload from the trucks in a defensive perimeter. We could hear rifle fire being aimed at the lead trucks and we could see the tracer rounds of a machine gun returning fire. After less than a quarter of an hour it went quiet and we were told to load back on the trucks. It was only general harassment by the VC. They were being opportunistic and did not engage us.

We stopped for the night outside a Marine artillery battery. We tried to sleep but its canons – 105 mm howitzers – were going off all night, and each time a round was fired, it seemed as if we were being raised a few inches off the ground. The artillery unit was set up just outside an abandoned village. We were camped right next to the village inside the perimeter of the artillery unit. During the night I heard a scurrying and got up and looked down the main street of the village to see what looked like thousands of rats running around.

The next morning our convoy continued and we arrived outside another village and set up our CP at around 11:00 am. Some of the villagers come around which made us very uncomfortable. Soon we received sniper fire through our new CP. The next day we received more sniper fire and it was returned. However, I understand that one of our line companies thought that we were shooting at them and opened fire on us in return. I was on the perimeter and my M14 had jammed with sand; I was trying to clean it by breaking it down into the three major groups (trigger assembly, stock and rifle group). Fortunately the misunderstanding was sorted out before I reassembled the rifle.

We were receiving so much sniper fire from the village that it was decided that we would move the CP to a graveyard that was a little way outside the village. We again established our CP and settled in. I found a nice grave that improvised as a fighting hole. It had a convenient concrete wall around it about two feet high. The center had a raised area for the body but there was about two feet of walking space around the actual raised grave site. I made a makeshift tent by using the wall of the grave and my poncho.

We were still receiving sniper fire through the CP. Luckily for us the sniper was not that great a shot. On the second morning in the graveyard, as I stood up I heard a round buzz by my head. I dropped to the ground and looked around the edge of the grave to see if whoever was firing was still there. He had shot at us enough for us to know where he was shooting from. The sniper would always shoot from the side of the graveyard where there were some very large boulders. Luckily, he had hurried his shot and missed me. He was obviously not a trained marksman. That day at around noon an Ontos moved in and positioned itself where it could get the sniper. The Ontos is a ferocious-looking tank-like vehicle with six 106 mm recoilless rifles mounted on it. It was sometimes called the "thing," "the six-gun," or the "pig." The Ontos had two large arms that held the six recoilless rifles. These arms were joined to a shallow turret. This entire assembly was cast in armored steel. The turret could turn forty degrees left and right. Since it was lighter than a tank it could move and manœuver very quickly. I had heard that the NVA was frightened of the Ontos and would avoid contact if possible. The sniper was probably VC rather than NVA but the effect was the same; we did not receive any more sniper fire from that area.

After several days of my sleeping in the graveyard the CP was moved. We got into our convoy and started off for a new location. As we were leaving, the last vehicle in the convoy was ambushed. The convoy stopped till the fight was over. It was not a serious engagement and no marines were killed. When we got to our new location a few hours later we could see the damage done. The back of the Mighty Mite jeep trailer was riddled with bullet holes.

On the way to the new CP location the convoy stopped and alongside our truck several Vietnamese girls stood waiting for our convoy to pass. One in particular caught my eye as she must have been on her way to something formal. She was dressed differently from the other girls, in a long, white formal áo dài. She was gorgeous with her long, black shining hair and her áo dài flowing in the gentle breeze. She was tall and was holding the cone-shaped hat that the Vietnamese country women wore. Her white áo dài had long sleeves and a long, high-necked silk tunic that had a slit at the sides to the waist. The áo dài was completed with baggy white pants that went over her feet. Even though she was covered totally she was very attractive. She looked up and our eyes met. She smiled and I nearly melted. It was one of those momentary things and I knew I would never see her again.

We unloaded at our new location, which was on the lawn of a public building in Tam Ky. It was a large lawn and some marines were already dug in. As we got off our deuce and a half truck to start to set up our CP, I noticed a dead Vietnamese man lying on the ground. He had been dead for a while since the flies were after him and he had a stench about him. I asked one of the marines there, "What's the scoop on the dead gook?" I learned that the day before he had infiltrated the perimeter and had been shot. They would not let the village across the fence have the body back to bury it. We were told that the Vietnamese believe that a person's spirit would roam around until the person has a proper burial. It seems that the marines here had had a rough few days as they had been mortared and attacked several times. The body was being held as an example.

We were digging our fighting holes and we were told to keep the children away from the fence. It was suspected that the children had been pretending to play on the other side of the fence and had identified where the fighting holes were, pacing off the distance for the mortaring on the previous nights.

As we finished digging our fighting holes, a terrible thunderstorm came up. It rained extremely hard with lightning striking all around. This seemed like a good time to bathe and most of us took out our soap and started to take advantage of the storm. The rain was so heavy that our fighting holes were totally filled with water in a matter of minutes. Two members of 3/5 were struck by lightning. One died instantly. They were both placed in a Mighty Mite jeep and were rushed by my fighting hole on their way to the corpsman. As they drove by, I saw that the marine who was alive was turning blue and looked disoriented as if he did not know where he was. They were both only in their skivvies, so they must have been bathing as well. I thought, what a terrible way to die. I guess there is no nice way for a young man to die, but you would think that in a war, if he had to die, it should be in combat.

The next two nights were uneventful and we started to take down the CP to head back for Chu Lai. As we were about leave, I was asked if I wanted to ride on one of the Ontos. I said I would, and loaded my gear into the deuce and a half truck with the other Comms platoon marines. Then I climbed quickly onto the front of the Ontos and sat down in between the two sets of guns with my M14 across my lap. As we started out I felt very secure sitting in the open since the Ontos struck fear into the hearts of its enemies. As we made our way back to Chu Lai we went across a lot of flat land; the rice paddies were beautiful, with mountains in the background. The countryside was like Jekyll and Hyde! One minute you were so seduced by the beauty of it all – it was like heaven with its peaceful scenes of farmers tending their fields with their water buffalo – and the next it was pure hell, with death and destruction all around you. I was fairly sure that it would be peaceful with me sitting on the Ontos.

CHAPTER THIRTY

GETTING READY TO MUSTER OUT

AFTER Operation Colorado we returned to the routine daily life of the temporary camp. We were engaged in putting telephone communication wire into the camp area. Since we were not on an operation we spent time going to the movies at the outdoor theater in Chu Lai, catching up on our inoculations and being involved in general busy work. I was feeling sick from the side effects of the many different vaccines that I received in updating my shot card. However, I still continued to work.

Sergeant Dorsey approached me and said that a couple of our line companies were going out and they needed a wireman to go with them, and that it was to be me. I objected. I was not feeling well from the inoculations; I had been passed over for sergeant; and I was very short (about to be released). One of the other senior sergeants heard what was going on and came over and said, "You can't send him out; he's too fucking short." I was surprised as sergeants don't normally interfere with each other. I said, "Sergeant Dorsey, with all due respect, it is not fair to send me out again; I'm about to go home." He looked at me and smiled, then walked away saying nothing. It was for Operation Jackson that took place between 24 August and 29 August and included Mike and Kilo companies from 3/5. I did not go out.

One of my Comms platoon friends knew someone in the air wing stationed at Chu Lai. He had an invitation to meet him at the air wing's non-commissioned officers' club. The next afternoon he and I wandered over at around 1600 hours. The facility at Chu Lai had a stream running through it and we had to cross a bridge to get to the air wing side from where our temporary camp was located. Vietnamese fishermen would launch their fishing boats from the mouth of the stream. It presented a possible danger since we could have been ambushed along the way.

We got to the air wing's NCO club and found that we were not allowed to take our M14s inside, so we hid them under a bush. It seemed as if the air wing lived a far better life than we did in the infantry. The NCO club was nicely appointed and we proceeded to get drunk with his friend. There was a live

Philippine band. Also in the club was a group of drunken Korean Marine NCOs. One of them wanted to sing a song with the band. He was allowed to sing and I remember him trying to imitate a train sound in one of his songs, much to the amusement of his fellows.

We sat and listened to my friend's story of how the perimeter fence of the air wing had been attacked and how the men on the perimeter were able to shoot the Vietcong as they were climbing over the fence. This young air wing marine was telling us how you could see your kill so it was confirmed. He went on to describe the time he had seen the man he killed climbing the fence. He did this with much pride. I thought back to Deckhouse 1 and the night of illumination, and the target that I had seen and shot at. I did not try to confirm if it was a kill or only an illusion caused by shadows. That clear shot that night during Deckhouse 1 was very different from the fire fights on the perimeter of Deckhouse 1, where we were firing into our fields of fire. At least 130 VC were killed attacking our command post on Deckhouse 1, so I could have had several kills. But why try and put notches on your weapon like a gunfighter? It is far more important for your fellow marines or yourself not to be a notch on the enemy's weapon yourself.

It was around 1900 hours when we started back to the temporary camp. We retrieved our M14s from under the bush outside the NCO club and began walking. My friend said, "He is a likable guy, but full of bullshit!" I replied, "He is a good man; I really enjoyed shooting the shit with him."

As we neared the temporary camp we came across several others of our corporal friends. We saw a light in the Comms tent and went to investigate. We all filed into the tent to find Captain Chalmers with an older looking marine who was wearing shiny, new, gold second lieutenant bars. We learned that he was a recently appointed mustang who had received his field promotion to become an officer.

It was polite conversation and by now we were totally drunk. However, as we sat and drank with Captain Chalmers and the new mustang officer, the mustang said, "Any Marine officer can kick the asses of any two Marine enlisted men!" In my mind I was thinking, "Aw shit, the wrong statement with this crowd!" He had the good sense to make his apologies and leave. Captain

Chalmers was a man who liked a challenge and would not drop the subject, and soon two of the corporals agreed to test the theory. There were about six or seven of us and we went out behind the tent for the fight. It soon became apparent that the theory was wrong and one of the other corporals joined in on Captain Chalmers side. Soon everyone was in it except me and one other marine. They would freely fight anyone; this was probably the result of the frustrations of the previous operations, which they were now venting. My friend Foley decided that I needed to be included and came for me. I wrestled him and pinned him down, but soon let him up without throwing a blow. He went back into the free-for-all.

After it was over, we all went back to our tents. The corporals involved who were living in my tent were bragging about the fight and how they had held up the honor of Marine enlisted men. I was feeling no pain and was laughing with my fellows. One of the young wiremen who had joined us as we left Okinawa, and had worked with me on all five combat operations, asked me, "Corporal Clubb, were you involved?" I said, "Yes." He said, "I never imagined you in a drunken brawl! You're always such a gentleman and a good marine." At that moment I felt like an old man and a little ashamed. Here was an eighteen-year-old marine who worked with me and looked up to me and I had let down his respect for me that night. The importance of being an NCO suddenly dawned on me and I realized that my four extra years of life were very significant. This young man had followed me and set up communications on all of our battalion landing team operations as well as Operation Colorado.

The next day, all of us who were about to muster out had to go through an interview with Captain Chalmers. I reported to him, saying, "Sir, Corporal Clubb reporting as ordered, sir." Captain Chalmers invited me to sit down in a chair positioned in front of his desk in the Comms platoon headquarters tent. I could see that Captain Chalmers was hurting from the fight the night before but he made a good effort at concealing his pain. Over the last few months in Vietnam I had talked about traveling to Europe and my desire to go to university and get a degree. It was common knowledge that I did not intend to "re-up." Captain Chalmers said, "The Corps is trying to keep those of you that have time in grade. Can I talk you into staying with the Corps?" I said, "No sir, I have plans." He said, "Yes, I know; we all know your ambitions but it is my job to try and convince you to stay in the Corps." I said, "Sir, I have my plans and will always be grateful to the Corps but re-enlisting is not part of those plans." He said, "Sorry to hear that you will not re-enlist; it has been a pleasure serving with you, Corporal." He and I then stood and we shook hands. Captain Chalmers said, "Good luck, Corporal Clubb." I stood at attention and said, "Sir, will that be all?" He said; "That will be all, Corporal." I replied with, "Aye aye, sir" and did an about face and left the tent.

At the beginning of September, Operation Jackson was over and 3/5 was moved out to take the place of one of the 7th Marines battalions on the Chu Lai defense perimeter. We were transported to the new area by deuce and a half trucks. The tents of the perimeter camp had wooden floors similar to the tents at Camp Matthews and we had sandbags around to reinforce the encampment. For the first time since Deckhouse 2 we were close to a village where interactions could take place. I saw for the first time young marines trying to get close to the young girls of the village. We who were about to muster out were only thinking of getting home.

When we wanted to buy something from the village we had to use MPCs (military payment certificates). These certificates were what we called funny money, but they were used in the same way as US dollar currency. The locals wanted to get greenbacks and an effort was made to prevent them from falling into their hands. There was a black market for greenbacks and the local people would always try to persuade us to pay with real US currency. If greenbacks were used, then the villagers would give goods at a better price.

Within a day after arriving at the new camp, those of us who were about to go back stateside turned in our weapons to the armory. I had to give up my trusty M14; it had been my faithful companion for nearly a year and I felt naked without my rifle. Also, we were now on the perimeter and there was more danger of being attacked so a rifle was handy.

They seemed to be in a hurry to get those of us mustering out through the process of going home. Especially since the 120-day involuntary extension was now over, and legally we had to be off active duty quickly. We also had to turn in all our jungle utilities as there was a shortage and the supplies people could reissue them. We were allowed to keep our jungle boots since it was felt that to reissue boots was not good.

I looked at Foley's eye, which was still black from the fight with Captain Chalmers. It was the blackest shiner I had ever seen. Foley must have been hit in the eye many times!

CHAPTER THIRTY-ONE

GOING STATESIDE

AFTER we had been on the outer perimeter of Chu Lai for only two days we were given our orders in a manila envelope and then we were taken with our sea bags to the Chu Lai airstrip. The majority of the group that was put together at the airstrip was mustering out. The ending of the 120-day involuntary extension caused more marines to be mustered out than normal. However, flying to Da Nang with us were several marines who had been in-country long enough to earn R&R and they were off for their week break somewhere outside of Vietnam. There must have been around thirty of us waiting to fly to Da Nang. We all boarded a C130 aircraft, leaving our sea bags sitting on the lowered boarding ramp. The crew threw a cargo net over the sea bags and strapped them down. We were seated on each side of the cargo bay on web seats. The pilot started the engines and the crew member in the cargo bay with us raised the ramp but not all the way. As we taxied down to the runway and started to take off we could see out of the gap left by the partially closed ramp. As the C130 lifted off we could see Chu Lai behind us as we gained altitude.

The flight was not very long, probably less than half an hour. We loaded off with our sea bags and waited for our transportation to take us to the ship that was to take us back to California. The marines who were going on R&R quickly disappeared. As we waited, it was amazing to see all the new troops arriving at Da Nang by air. We all felt sorry for these green troops. They had received less training than we had as the Marine Corps had shortened boot camp and some marines were now being drafted. I never thought that I would see draftees in the Marines since we had always been a voluntary armed service. I heard that during WWII some marines had been drafted, but I felt it would water down the effectiveness of the units. I guess the failure to keep us older marines in the Corps had caused it to rely on the draft to keep up its manpower. We looked at the new replacements and shook our heads. They did not know what they were getting into.

We were soon loaded onto deuce and a half trucks and were transported through town. Da Nang was very different from the streets of Okinawa or the Philippines. I felt uncomfortable without my M14 as we rode through the streets. People were going about their business and ignored the convoy. The convoy took about the same amount of time to get us to a riverside landing as the C130 flight had done to get us to Da Nang. We loaded onto boats and were transported out to the USS *General W. H. Gordon* (AP-117), anchored in Da Nang Bay. As we boarded the ship we realized that there were quite a few marines already aboard but also that we were not the last to arrive. I looked at Foley's eye, which was still black from the fight with Captain Chalmers. It remained the blackest shiner I had ever seen.

~~

I learned that normally marines who mustered out were flown home, but since there were so many of us to discharge, a ship had to be used for the September batch. The *General W. H. Gordon* was very comfortable compared with other military ships I had been aboard. It had been used by the army as a troop transport for a while. It had a good arrangement of bunks and the mess deck was far better than that of most ships. By the end of the day we finally got underway and I felt very mellow and relaxed.

Our first and only port of call was in Okinawa. We were to stay there for twenty-four hours to take on provisions for the Pacific Ocean passage. This gave us our final liberty in a foreign port before returning to the US. We all went ashore to see some of the old hangouts that we used to frequent in Koza. I did not try to find a woman and spent the liberty with one of my married friends, who was not interested in being unfaithful to his wife, being so close to getting home. I had promised my friend McKay that I would buy him a Seiko watch and mail it to him when I got home. So I located a watch shop and bought the Seiko for him. We went to several bars before returning to the ship. As we got back we discovered that the ship had been shaken down for contraband; several AK-47s, a lot of ammo and some jungle utilities had been found.

After our night of liberty, and with massive hangovers, we got underway again and learned that we would not stop in

Hawai'i but go directly to San Diego. We were taking a more northerly passage. The ship was traveling at a good speed so we would not have to endure the more than one month passage that we had experienced coming over to Okinawa.

Two days after the ship left Okinawa we had a "short arms inspection." This took place at 0300 hours. We were woken and then filed by a group of corpsmen who had blocked off the head. They had each of us hold our penis and skin it back. They were looking for "the drip"; gonorrhea, or clap, as it is known to the enlisted ranks. (Officers contract social diseases; enlisted men get the clap.) Those that had a wet penis head had to give a urine sample and the rest of us were allowed to have a pee and go back to our bunks to sleep for the rest of the night.

The result of the inspection was that twenty-three confirmed cases of gonorrhea were found. A very sad case was that of one of our married marines who was trying to figure out what to tell his wife about how he had caught the clap. Since the passage was to be fast, it looked as if he would not have the more than two weeks needed to cure the disease before arriving stateside. I saw him looking over the side of the ship with tears in his eyes. It was ironic that a man who had had to fight for his life was in such emotional conflict as he was going home. The ship's chaplain and the corpsmen were working with him, trying to sort him out.

Life settled into the normal shipboard routine for marines; killing time and staying out of the way of the sailors running the ship. We would chat with each other about our plans and our families. Life was very pleasant indeed. As the ship made progress we were experiencing something similar to jet lag. We found that we were getting up earlier and going to sleep earlier. It was a weird sensation to have the day reverse on us. The mess deck was open for us to sit around and chat twenty-four hours a day. The ship's company was good as we were on our way home.

We passed the International Dateline and regained the day that we had lost on our way to Asia. The experience was uneventful and in fact was hardly noticed.

I met a German national who had come from Europe to be a marine. He was returning home after his combat experience. As I had always wanted to go to Europe, I questioned him a lot about his life there. He suggested that the two of us pair up and become gigolos on the Riviera. He told me about all the rich old ladies there who took on young men. It sounded good to me at the time but reality soon set in and I returned to my university plans.

For a couple of days we hit rough seas and for the first time on a passage I felt that I might become seasick. Going north we had encountered a storm and the ship was really rocking. I went and lay in my bunk to avoid the embarrassment of throwing up. The passage from Okinawa took less than two weeks and we arrived in San Diego on a late September afternoon.

CHAPTER THIRTY-TWO

HOME AT LAST

THE ship docked in San Diego and we were offloaded and taken to the Marine Corps Recruit Depot. We occupied several Quonset huts that were used for recruit training. After settling into my new bunk bed I decided that it was too late to go home to La Puente. A couple of the junior Comms marines (they were on three-year enlistments and were still lance corporals) suggested that I go to Tijuana with them for drinks. I said that I would but told them that I wanted to go home the next day so had to get back early.

We all dressed in our civilian clothes and drew our liberty cards. It was a short bus ride to the border and we started going from club to club drinking cheap Corona beer. After a couple of hours I told them I had to go. They both said that they would stay but did not want to keep all their money and gave part of it to me for safekeeping. I returned to the Quonset hut, had my shower and went to sleep.

At morning formation we were told that we had a twenty-four hour liberty, and that all those of us who were corporals and met the criteria for promotion to sergeant E-5 were to be promoted, backdated to 1 September 1966. Our units had had no right to hold back our promotions because we had opted not to re-enlist. The news of the promotion was like natural justice. It had been hard for us to see junior corporals promoted over our heads.

Both of my two friends with whom I had been in Tijuana the previous night were missing from morning formation. After formation I was called in and told that they had got into a fight with a couple of squids and were in the Tijuana jail. They had told the police that I would help them since I had their money and could cover bail. I agreed to go and bail them out and went to the Military Police to learn the procedure for doing this.

I got into my civilian clothes, drew my liberty card and instead of going home to La Puente I went to Tijuana to free my friends. Arriving in Tijuana, I followed the MP's instructions on how to locate the jail. It must have been a common practice to pay fines to get marines (or squids) out of jail. I used part of the money that I was holding for them to bail them out and gave them back the balance of what I was holding. I then crossed the border back into San Diego and started to hitchhike to La Puente.

It was about 5:00 pm when I walked down the road to my home on Hutchcroft Street in La Puente. No one knew that I was coming home. When I got to the house I just walked in. All who were there were very excited to see me back. When my dad returned from work he did something very much unexpected, he grabbed me and hugged me and kissed me on my cheek. My mother was in tears; I had never seen her so happy.

I drove to the local liquor store to buy champagne to celebrate. We started drinking bottles of champagne purchased with some of the pay that I had drawn. We went through twenty bottles of champagne and one of rosé, which I must have bought by accident, being so drunk. I remember lying on my bed, with one of the neighbors, who was Mexican, playing a guitar and singing in Spanish to me while I was passing in and out. My whole family and most of our neighbors were sitting around me. I was nearly paralyzed from the amount of wine that I had drunk.

My sisters Sue and Sandy agreed to drive me back to the MCRD for the morning formation and we left at 4:00 am. I was lying in the back seat of my sister Sue's car with a bucket that I kept vomiting into. The previous night had really taken its toll. We arrived at the MCRD at around 6:30 am and I quickly said good bye to my sisters and rushed in to get changed for morning formation.

As announced in the previous morning's formation, those of us who qualified were going to get our formal promotions to sergeant E-5 that morning. I changed into my summer khaki class B uniform for the presentation of the promotion certificates. After formation, all of us who were to be promoted quickly lined up in front of an office on the building side of the MCRD, waiting to be presented with our certificates. There were around fifteen to twenty of us who had been held back. My turn came and I reported to the officer doing the presentation, "Sir, Corporal Clubb reporting as ordered, sir." He handed me the certificate and shook my hand saying, "Congratulations Sergeant Clubb." Even my delicate condition from the previous night could not dampen the feeling of pride and euphoria that overtook me.

After returning to my Quonset hut I took all my summer uniforms to the laundry to have my new sergeant stripes sewn on. The rest of the day was taken up with another exit interview by a group that was trying to get us to re-enlist.

I was looking in the newspaper classifieds for a car and saw an Austin Healy Sprite for sale for US$300. I had always wanted a sports car so I arranged a meeting with the owner at the motor vehicle department. The next day after morning formation I went directly to the motor vehicle department. I wanted to see the car and buy it if it was in reasonable shape. I was still in my summer uniform from morning formation.

The car was reasonable and drove well. We were by then inside and I was giving the owner money for the car after we had transferred the title to my name. He pointed to my ribbons and asked about them. I said that I'd just returned from Vietnam. He replied, "You're one of those people who were over there killing women and babies, then!" I did not know what to say. I felt like hitting him but that would have been a wrong move. My face must have been very red as I was so angry and did not understand why someone would say such a thing. It was all I could do to control myself. This was the first lesson learned on returning home. I realized that those of us who had served in Vietnam were not very popular. I could not understand this, since I never did anything that I was ashamed of while in-country. I was proud that I had served with the Marines. I kept my cool and just walked away, got into my new car and drove off. To me he was scum and not worth going to jail over!

My country was very polarized! We were not greeted as returning heroes as the servicemen of WWII had been. We were mostly from poor families and followed the natural course to serve our country in the armed forces. The military had provided a job and the chance to learn a trade for those of us that chose that route. The military, for young enlisted men, was like a poor man's college. Those of us who had served were being treated as if we were criminals by some people. We were true examples of the old Marine saying that "shit flows down hill."

On the morning of 3 October 1966, I was released from active duty and returned to civilian life.

EPILOGUE

AFTER leaving active duty on 4 October 1966, life of course went on. However, that is a different story.

The Corps has been one of the greatest influences on my life. Looking back, the Corps was my home, my mentor and the inspiration for me to get on with my life. It took a teenager with a low opinion of himself, who was very disturbed by a disrupted family life, and gave him purpose and pride. I still needed greater maturity, however, and I have made mistakes since leaving the Corps that have been very painful lessons in life.

I listened to the naval psychiatrist and did not go back to live with my family. My mother tried very hard to get me to return home but I did not wish to fall again into the disruptive daily life that I had experienced as a youth.

In 1980, I lost my mom to lung cancer when she was fifty-two; she smoked two packs of cigarettes a day. I loved her dearly; she was one of nature's lost souls. She blindly loved her man to the point that she neglected her children. I was able to see her a few hours before her death and she made peace with me over leaving me at the age of three. My dad fell apart at Mom's funeral and was crying uncontrollably. My brother Doug and I had to support him by standing on each side of him holding his hands throughout the ceremony.

My grandparents both passed away the year after Mom, leaving only Dad as parent or grandparent. My grandmother passed first and Papa died a week later, I'm sure of heartbreak. After so many years together, they were one. Papa could not function without Grandma. I was able to talk to Papa on the telephone from Hong Kong for a few minutes before his death. His voice was frail and he was not speaking coherently. Gone was the strength of the man that I loved the most in my life. He was a true role model in my childhood. It was very painful to hear him speak. He told me that Grandma had gone to heaven and he was going to join her soon. Papa had grown old and had come to grips with his religious doubts by surrendering to pure blind faith. I often wonder what Papa would have been if given different circumstances. He had the questioning mind of a scholar.

After Mom's funeral Dad went off and spent our mother's funeral money on a young, thirty-five-year-old woman. I never forgave him and never spoke to him again. He died seventeen years later from an intestinal blockage that became septic. I wrote the eulogy for his funeral, which my brother David read, but I did not attend. Looking back, I think of the words that I recently saw on a church marquee in Hilo, Hawai'i: "Forgiveness is better for the forgiver than the forgiven." I could have handled my father's passing with a little more sensitivity. The death of my dad left me feeling alone in the world. I have filled this vacuum of loneliness with love for my family of three boys, wives and friends.

Marilyn and I exchanged letters several times after I first returned to the US. I was thinking of joining the Air Force and had been offered a package by a recruiter to join at the same pay grade as when I left active duty with the Marines, and my choice of duty station worldwide. I was thinking I could select Clark Air Force Base in the Philippines and could move Marilyn close to me. After writing and telling Marilyn of this plan, I received a letter from her saying that she was glad that I had lived through the last of my combat operations and that I should now start a new life in the US. This hurt since I was willing to move closer to her. My mother told me that I should have married her while overseas. I told her that she was a bar girl and that once a girl fell into the trade she rarely escaped. She was shocked since I had always painted Marilyn as a perfect woman.

I'm sure that my relationship with Marilyn was good for me, even with the pain of the betrayal. I think that she loved me as well, but had to get on with her life and had probably found someone else. Hopefully, she and her son got out of the trap she was in. She had told me that her family had disowned her but was always willing to accept her money and would even ask her for it! She was a victim of economics. She sold the only thing that she had that was marketable and had to do it before age had set in and she was no longer desirable. In the end, I decided not to go into the Air Force and never heard from Marilyn again.

After going to work for the Bank of America's Data Processing Division in Los Angeles, I met Cheryl Aikiko Suzumoto, a lovely Japanese-American girl from Hawai'i. I started to work for the Bank less than two weeks after leaving the Marines. Cheryl was the general manager's secretary. We were both living on our own and were very soon dating. We married on 4 July 1967. She was my best friend and we really loved each other's company. The time with Cheryl in Los Angeles was the happiest I had ever had in my life.

At the start of the Christmas season of 1967, her father committed suicide. He had recently gone through a divorce from Cheryl's mom. They had found a family photo album open where he was looking at his family before hanging himself. This nearly killed Cheryl. I remember the pain it caused her when she learned of her father's fate. She cried for several days. We flew to Honolulu for the funeral. After we returned to Los Angeles, I agreed to move to Hawai'i since she was hurt and very homesick. We moved to Honolulu in the summer of 1968. Neither marriage nor Hawai'i was in my original plans when I left active duty. However, the thought of living in Hawai'i struck a positive chord in me and sounded like a new adventure.

I enjoyed Hawai'i and spent the majority of my time there working for the Bank of Hawai'i, in its information technology department. Since I was now married and working, I could not study full-time. I was able to get into Leeward Community College (LCC) and started to study part-time in the evenings. After attending for a semester, I was asked if I would teach a course entitled Systems Analysis and Design for the college as they could not find anyone else with experience to do so. By now, I was a systems analyst, which gave me the necessary experience. I had never lectured before and I jumped at the chance of the part-time work. Over the next few years I did a lot of part-time courses for LCC and enjoyed the work. I finished my Associate Degree in Liberal Arts in December 1971.

In Hawai'i, both Cheryl and I were very different people. Cheryl was someone who enjoyed home life. We did not cling to each other as we had in Los Angeles. We agreed to have a child and Christopher was born on 3 August 1970. I love the outdoors and adventure and I felt very tied down. I guess that I inherited some of my dad's rolling-stone personality. I bought a large sailboat and wanted to take the family on an around-the-world cruise. Cheryl would not buy into this idea. I did not wish to be like my dad and abandon my family, so in the end I sold the boat. Around this time, Alex Haley's book *Roots* was published, and Cheryl jokingly once told me I had "root rot!" The problem was amplified since I was working full-time, lecturing part-time and attending night school almost every night of the week. In December 1975 I finished my Bachelor of Arts degree in Psychology, having studied at the Manoa campus part-time through their continuing education program.

In the mid-1970s the once-a-month weekends that I spent with the Marine Corps Active Reserve added to the time I was away from home and the problems this caused. In Honolulu I was part of 4th Force Recon Company. That lasted only for about three months when I left the Marine Corps Active Reserves for the Coast Guard Active Reserve, with the objective of getting a reserve commission. I really enjoyed the Active Reserves and made it to Data Processor First Class (E-6) in the Coast Guard Reserve. The reserve commission never panned out as in 1977 I applied for and was offered a post in Hong Kong, teaching at the Hong Kong Polytechnic. I had to give up my Active Reserve military career. Had I stayed in Hawai'i I'm sure that I would eventually have received my commission.

I was relocated by the Hong Kong Polytechnic to Hong Kong in August 1977. This brought on the destruction of my marriage. Cheryl was not a Hong Kong fan. Hong Kong in the mid- to late 1970s was a Third World British Colony, in character an elitist labor-intensive economy and not the vibrant city of today. To her credit, Cheryl did come with me and lived in Hong Kong for nine months. We were divorced the following year.

In my thirties, I was a very ambitious, self-centered man. I look back on the divorce and the pain that I caused to everyone involved and feel that I was unfair. I thought that I had the individualism that we in the West treasure so much. However, I was mostly concerned with my own selfishness rather than the good of my family. I now realize the difference between individualism and selfishness.

I remember meeting my then eight-year-old son, Christopher, in Japan during his Christmas 1978 school break when he fell asleep on my arm as we rode on the bus from Narita Airport into Tokyo for a tour. It brought tears to my eyes since I missed him so much. We toured Tokyo and I took him to see snow in Nikko. We had a great time and I cherished being with him.

I met my wife of the last thirty-one years (as of the time of writing this), Helen Ng Siu Ha, in the general office of the Computing Department at Hong Kong Polytechnic. Helen was a clerical officer. After the start of my second two-year contract with the Polytechnic, Helen left to join Cathay Pacific Airways as a flight attendant. She had worked for Cathay Pacific for a little more than nine months when we were married. Helen is thirteen years younger than me and I was accused of robbing the cradle by my former Bank of Hawai'i friends. Through her Cathay benefits I am now well traveled. We have two fine sons, Ian and Samuel. Helen has shown great patience with me. She prizes her family and loves her boys very much. She has worked hard to provide for them the childhood that neither of us had.

I continued to work in Southeast Asia until I reached the mandatory retirement age of sixty-five in 2009. While working, I continued my formal studies and received a PhD from the University of Sunderland in 2002. After retiring, I purchased a macadamia nut and coffee farm on the Island of Hawai'i. I still maintain a residence in Hong Kong, commuting between Hong Kong and Hawai'i. My sister Sandy and her husband Joe tend to the farm during my absences.

Last but not least, I think of my beloved Corps!

The individuals whom I served with in my several years of active duty were from many different backgrounds. We all entered boot camp as strangers but all who graduated were marines. Many of my cohorts died in Vietnam and other far-off places. I am lucky that I have lived to tell, finally, about my experiences. To my brothers who have passed, either in combat or having lived to a ripe old age, I salute you.

So what is a marine?

A marine has what it takes to go through the initiation process of the required training to win the cherished title of "marine". Upon winning the title every marine considers the honor and legacy of the Corps as his personal and sacred trust and for the rest of his life he will defend and protect the honor and legacy of the Corps. The title "marine" is not given but has to be fought for and won. Once a marine has won that coveted title, it sparks an eternal flame of devotion and fierce pride in his soul. The Corps is neither a social club nor a fraternal organization and it never pretends to be. The Corps is a brotherhood of warriors. Once in this brotherhood, for your remaining days you are a marine first, regardless of age, race, creed, color, sex or national origin. It is a brotherhood with roots as far back as 1775.[5] It is a brotherhood that has never lost it colors in battle. The Corps does not include in its vocabulary the words, "retreat", "can't" or "lose". All battles are entered into with the sole objective to win.

I would like to close with the words of some senior Military officers.

General Douglas MacArthur, US Army; outskirts of Seoul, 21 September 1950: "There is not a finer fighting organization in the world."

Major General Frank E. Lowe, US Army; Seoul, Korea, 26 January 1952: "The safest place in Korea was right behind a platoon of Marines. Lord, how they could fight!"

General H. Norman Schwarzkopf, US Army, Riyadh, Saudi Arabia, 27 February 1991: "I can't say enough about the two Marine divisions. If I use words like brilliant, it would really be an under-description of the absolutely superb job they did in breaching the so-called impenetrable barrier. . .. Absolutely superb operation, a textbook, and I think it'll be studied for many, many years to come as the way to do it."

General James F. Amos, 35th Commandant of the Marines: "A marine is a marine. ... there's no such thing as a former marine.... you'll always be a marine because you went to Parris Island, San Diego or the hills of Quantico. There's no such thing as a former marine."[6]

And finally, here's what General Louis H. Wilson, Commandant of the Marine Corps, said in a Toast given at the 203rd Marine Corps Birthday Ball at Camp Lejueune, N.C. 1978:

> The wonderful love of a beautiful maid,
> The love of a staunch true man,
> The love of a baby, unafraid,
> Have existed since time began.

---

[5] http://en.wikipedia.org/wiki/Tun_Tavern
[6] Reported in *Seahorse Magazine,* Volume #, 19 April 2011 as referenced in "Medals of America DD-214 blog", http://blog.medalsofamerica.com/only-marines-former-marines-2/

But the greatest of loves, The quintessence of loves,
even greater than that of a mother,
Is the tender, passionate, infinite love,
of one drunken marine for another.

"Semper Fidelis!"

EARLY RESPONSE TO *SEMPER FI*

I first met Lee in Hong Kong on or about 1987. At the time, I was a US Secret Service agent from the Honolulu, Hawai'i Field Office. The Honolulu Field Office has supervision over all Secret Service operations from Honolulu to Pakistan. Lee and I were both into martial arts and we met at the Hong Kong Police Aikido Club. As I am 6'2" and Lee is 6'4", we were immediately paired up.

We found that we had more in common than just height; namely, we were both born in 1944, I was born in March and Lee in June, Lee had resided in Hawai'i where I was currently stationed, and most importantly, we were fellow Marines. I was a helicopter pilot and, while in Vietnam, I flew the CH 46 Sea Knight with HMM 165, the White Knights. I served in Vietnam in 1972 and flew missions off of the USS Tripoli, LPH 10 and USS New Orleans, LPH 11.

There is a bond between Marines that is eloquently explained in this book. This is the story of an American who came from a humble background, who had a great love for his country and who put his life on the line for it. The book explains how the Corps transformed his attitude, self confidence, and personality. It gave him the inspiration to become a successful person and PhD, a degree that is attained by fewer than three per cent of the American population.

If you have no military background this book will inspire you, if you have a military background it will bring back memories of your own service, if you are a Marine, "Semper Fi!"

Alan J. Zygowicz, Major USMC, Special Agent in Charge Hong Kong Office, US Secret Service 1996-1999

EARLY RESPONSE TO *SEMPER FI*

Dr. Lee Clubb has chronicled his life experiences, which include a difficult upbringing and a life-changing term of service in the Marine Corps. His book is a tribute to what the Corps has meant to thousands of young men, who believed that this path, although difficult, would lead them into manhood and a better future. Any prospective recruit who wonders what marine boot camp is like will find it highly informative. On the other hand, *Semper Fi* is bound to rekindle memories for any veteran reading it. This is why I had initial reservations about reading it! I served as an 0311 (rifleman) with the first Marine Division near Danang in 1968 and 1969. Like many war veterans, I have found the best coping mechanism is to put the experience behind me, and whenever possible, out of mind. Service in the Marine Corps can be extremely challenging, as Lee Clubb so clearly describes. Marines frequently say that, never in a million years, would they want to serve with the Corps again; but they also say that they would not trade their experience for a million dollars. As an aging Vet, I am encouraged that, even today, the very best young people in our nation are willing to serve in all branches of our armed services. I am especially proud of those who elect to serve in the Marine Corps. "Semper Fi!"

Kelley Douglas, MD, PhD

GLOSSARY

The following terms are used in this book; not all are specific to the Marine Corps.

3/5	3rd Battalion 5th Marines.
782 gear	Marine Corps-issue field equipment consisting of packs, web gear (webbing), half shelter, tent poles, canteen and cover, entrenching tool, cartridge belt, magazine pouches, first aid kit, etc. (Form 782 was the form to be filled out to draw the issue.)
Ammo	Ammunition.
Ao dai	Vietnamese women's traditional long-sleeved, ankle-length slit tunic worn over trousers.
As you were!	Resume what you were doing; correction.
Assholes to bellybuttons	A tight formation; one behind the other.
Bazooka	Antitank rocket launcher.
BCE	Before the Christian Era.
B service uniform	Khaki summer uniform
Beachmaster	An amphibious beach party unit.
Bleachers	Tiered rows of seats.
Blousing	Using a garter-like piece of elastic to secure utility trouser cuffs.
BLT	Battalion landing team
Boondocks	Rugged, isolated back country.
Boot	Slang for recruit.
Boot camp	Training camp with harsh discipline for recruits.
Brig	Prison or place of confinement aboard ship or ashore at a Marine Corps or naval station.
Brig rat	A person who has served much brig time, a habitual offender.
Brig chaser	Person assigned to escort prisoners.
Butts	The place where targets are located in a shooting range.
C4	Composition 4; a common variety of the plastic explosive known as Composition C. Plastic: because it can be molded.
C Company	One company in a battalion: C for Charlie (Alpha, Bravo, Charlie…)
Canteen	Part of 782 gear, a bottle to carry water in.
Casual section	Unit of Marines Corps where marines await reassignment.
Catwalk	Narrow, metal, grated walkway outside the main ship's structure and exposed to the elements.
Chin-up	A strength training exercise for the upper body using a parallel bar.
Chit	Written authorization or receipt.
Chow	Food.
Chow hall	Mess hall; a place where service personnel eat.

Chuck	Black marine's term for white marine.
Click	One notch of adjustment on a rifle's sight.
C-rations (C-rats)	Combat rations; canned food for the field. Each ration consists of one meal for one marine.
Comms	Communications
CP	Command post.
Corpsman	Navy medic serving with Marines.
Deck	Floor.
Deuce-and-a-half	Two-and-a-half-ton truck.
DI	Drill Instructor
DMZ	Demilitarized zone – in the case of Vietnam, the area that divided North and South Vietnam; the 17th parallel.
Deedee (Viet.)	Leave; go; get away.
Doc	A medical person; navy corpsman or navy doctor.
Donned and clear	Fitted to the face and free of gas.
Dope	Increments of windage and elevation on a rifle's adjustable sight.
Double time	Quickly; at a run.
Dress blues	Marines' blue uniform jacket and trousers with red trim.
Dry fire	Practice.
Dry run	Practice.
Duck walk	To "walk" in a squatting position.
EE8	Standard field telephone of WWII used extensively in Vietnam.
Entrenching tool	Small folding field shovel.
Fantail	The stern overhang of a ship.
Field day	General clean-up of barracks. A day or portion of a day set aside for top-to-bottom cleaning of an area; also as a verb for the act of conducting a field day.
Field strip	Disassemble; take apart. To disassemble a piece of ordnance or weapon to the major part groups for routine cleaning or lubricating; to strip cigarette butts to their filters before throwing away.
Fire in the hole!	Warning that explosives are about to be detonated.
Fire team	The most basic Marine infantry unit; consists of a fire team leader (usually a corporal or lance corporal), an automatic rifleman (armed with an M14 with an automatic fire selector), an assistant automatic rifleman (who humps the extra ammunition) and a rifleman (who goes out to try and draw fire so that everyone else can see if the coast is clear). There are three fire teams to a Marine rifle squad.
FMF	Fleet Marine Force. The operational forces of the Corps, as opposed to reserve or supporting establishment. Combined general and special purpose forces within the US Navy designed to engage offensive amphibious or expeditionary warfare and for defensive maritime employment.

Force Recon	Force Reconnaissance Companies. In the 1960s and 1970s, each Marine Division had one Force Recon Company that was broken into 4-man teams. Each man was SCUBA and parachute trained. There were normally deployed behind enemy lines (from a surface ship, submarine, or parachuting in). We used to say "one for shooting, two for looting and one to take the pictures".
Gear	Equipment.
Grinder	The large parade field in the center of the Marine Corps Recruit Depot, San Diego, where Marine drill instructors drilled and drilled their boot charges.
Grunt	An infantryman; Low-ranking enlisted man employed doing manual labor.
Gunny	Gunnery Sergeant, the 7th enlisted rank in the USMC. Logistics and operations chief of a company of Marines.
HMM	Helicopter Marine Medium.
H&S Company	Headquarters and Service Company: Headquarters consists of the commanding officer of the battalion and his staff; Services are in the S (service) sections. S1 Administration and personnel, S2 Intelligence, S3 operations and training; S4 Logistics and Supply, S5 plans and S6 communications.
Hatch	Door.
Head	Toilet.
High-and-tight	Standard marine haircut; shaved sides and short on top.
Honcho (Jap.)	Boss; man in charge.
Hump	To march; to carry; to be burdened with.
Ice plant	Short plants of Family Aizoaceae which grow in dry conditions and are used to stabilize soil.
Incoming!	Hostile fire being received!
Irish pennant	Threads dangling from clothing indicating unkempt appearance.
ITR	Infantry Training Regiment.
Interlocking fire	Covering an area with small arms fire so that the firings from two or more pieces overlap.
Junk-on-the-bunk	Complete clothing and equipment (782 gear) inspection (also known as Things-on-the-Springs) laid out on the rack.
Klick	Kilometer.
Leave	Annual Vacation. Normally one month (30 days) leave per year of service. Leave is given in days.
Liberty	Authorized free time ashore or off station, not counted as leave. Liberty is given in hours. Could be Cinderella liberty (ends at 23:00 hours or mid-night, normally given when stationed on ships that are in port) or a 24, 48, 72, & 96 (i.e. hours), the standard liberties of one, two, three, or four days. For a weekend you would get a 48.
LPH	Landing platform helicopter; a navy ship that carries helicopters from which they operate; also carries segments of a BLT.
Lock and load	Arm and ready your weapon with the weapon's safety on.

LZ	Landing zone; an area where a helicopter can land. If it is a "hot" LZ there will be enemy fire.
M14 rifle	Standard issue automatic US rifle from 1959 to 1970.
Maggie's drawers	Red flag used on the rifle range to signify missing the target.
Mail call	Time when mail is distributed to assembled service personnel.
MCRD	Marine Corps Recruit Depot
Medevac	Timely and efficient medical evacuation of the wounded from the battlefield.
Mess hall	See chow hall.
MPC	Military payment certificate; while in-country (Vietnam), used in lieu of greenbacks.
MOS	Military occupation specialty (assigned job specialty).
Motor pool	Military vehicle parking lot; A group of military vehicles dispatched for use when needed.
Mustang	Enlisted man who becomes an officer.
Muster out	Leave or discharge from military service.
NCO	Non-commissioned officer; a position of authority such as a corporal or sergeant achieved by promotion through the ranks.
NVA	North Vietnamese Army.
Ontos	Armored tracked vehicle mounting six 106 mm recoilless rifles.
Piece	Rifle.
Platoon	In the United States Marine Corps, rifle (AKA infantry) platoons are led by a platoon commander, usually a second lieutenant, aided by an NCO.
Pogey bait	Candy; sweets. (For derivation of the term, see: www.urbandictionary.com/define.php?term=pogey%20bait)
Police up	Clean up an area.
Post	A place where someone is on duty or carrying out a job.
PRC-10	A back-packable radio transceiver; pronounced *prick ten*.
PT	Physical training; exercise.
Pugil stick	Heavily padded poles which Marine recruits spar with to simulate rifle and bayonet combat.
Purple heart	Heart-shaped military decoration awarded to those who have been wounded or killed while serving since 1917 with the US military.
Quonset hut	Prefabricated building with a semi-cylindrical corrugated roof. Based on the British Nissen hut of WWI. First made at Quonset Point, Rhode Island.
R&R	Rest and recuperation; a short leave from the war zone to an area where alcohol, clean living quarters and recreation might be found.
Rack	Bed, bunk.
Rappel	Descend from cliff or helicopter by rope.
Receiver	Rifle chamber
Recon	Exploring beyond the area occupied by friendly forces to gain information about enemy forces or features of the environment. See "Force Recon."
Round	Bullet, artillery or mortar shell.
S2	Intelligence component of a battalion. (See H&S company.)

Skosh (Jap.)	Small, short, a little bit.
Scuttlebutt	Rumor. Can also mean drinking fountain. The word derives from a scuttled (holed) wooden cask/butt which in the time of sailing ships would be used to store fresh water. Sailors would gather round the butt to drink and gossip.
Sea bag	Used to carry one's personal belongings. Cf. "Duffle bag" is an Army term not used by Marines; A large canvas bag into which sailors and marines stuff their entire issue of uniforms and personal items when being transferred.
Shit bird	Messy or undisciplined; a fuck up.
Shop Chief	NCO in charge of the repair section and technicians of the communication platoon of an H&S company.
Short	Nearing the end of a tour of duty or enlistment.
Short round	Ordnance which is landing short of the intended target.
Sick bay	Infirmary or other medical facility aboard ship or aid stations ashore.
Sight in	Adjustments made to rifle sights so that bullet hits the target.
Skeet range	Range where a clay target is thrown from a trap to simulate the flight of a bird.
Skivvies	Underwear
Skuzzy	Dirty; gross.
SLF	Special Landing Force; In the 1960s, the designation of the combined USMC BLT and a Helicopter Marine Medium (HMM) squadron plus other reinforcements. The SLF was assigned to the Seventh Fleet Amphibious Ready Group. While at sea, the SLF was under the command of the Navy. In our case, the Seventh Fleet. Once ashore it was under it own command or under the command of whoever the SLF was supporting. The SLF regularly conducted amphibious operations across Vietnamese beaches into areas of suspected VC and NVA activity.
Smoking lamp	When the smoking lamp is lit it is alright to smoke, when it is out smoking is prohibited.
Smoker	Boxing match.
Smokey Bear hat	Brown campaign cover (hat) worn by drill instructors, so named because of their similarity to the hat worn by Smokey Bear the US Forest Service mascot.
Snap in	Conduct sighting in or aiming exercises with an unloaded weapon.
Splib	Black marine's term for black marine.
Squad bay	Living quarters for a recruit platoon; consists of a large open space where bunk beds are set up, a head, a drill instructor's hut and a small meeting area. Also, any open living space for marines.
Squared away	Neat, orderly, organized.
Squid (derog.)	Sailor.
Stand by!	Prepare!
Standby	Waiting status.
Strapping in	Use of the rifle strap and proper body positions to steady the rifle.

Suck, the	The suck; miserable situation or place, often used to describe the Marine Corps or a combat zone.
Swab	Mop.
Tracer rounds	Bullets or shells whose course is made visible by a trail of flames or smoke; used to help in aiming.
Undesirable discharge	Discharge commonly given to service members found guilty of "Sexual Perversion." or service member who could not adapt to military life.
USMC	United States Marine Corps.
Utilities	Olive-drab field uniform; fatigues.
VC	Viet Cong.
Word, the	Confirmed official information; the straight scoop.
Zulu time	Greenwich Mean Time.

WRITE TO US!

We are interested to read your response to
Lee Clubb's *Semper Fi*
and any other of our publications.
Please write to our email address, proverse@netvigator.com,
giving us a few sentences which you are willing for us to publish,
giving your comments on this book.
If what you write is chosen to be included
in our E-Newsletter or website,
we will select another title published by Proverse
and send you a complimentary copy.
Please include your name, email address and mailing address
when you write to us, and state whether or not we may cut or
edit your comments for publication.
We will use your initials to attribute your comments.

ABOUT PROVERSE HONG KONG

Proverse Hong Kong is based in Hong Kong with long-term and expanding regional and international connections.

Proverse has published novels, novellas, fictionalized autobiography, non-fiction (including autobiography, biography, history, memoirs, sport, travel narratives), single-author poetry collections, children's, teens / young adult and academic books. Other interests include diaries, and academic works in the humanities, social sciences, cultural studies, linguistics and education. Some Proverse books have accompanying audio texts. Some are translated into Chinese.

Proverse welcomes authors who have a story to tell, wisdom, perceptions or information to convey, a person they want to memorialize, a neglect they want to remedy, a record they want to correct, a strong interest that they want to share, skills they want to teach, and who consciously seek to make a contribution to society in an informative, interesting and well-written way. Proverse works with texts by non-native-speaker writers of English as well as by native English-speaking writers.

The name, "Proverse", combines the words "prose" and "verse" and is pronounced accordingly.

THE PROVERSE PRIZE

The Proverse Prize, an annual international competition for an unpublished book-length work of fiction, non-fiction, or poetry, was established in January 2008. It is open to all who are at least eighteen on the date they sign the entry form. Unusually for a competition of this nature, there is no restriction based on nationality, residence or citizenship.

The objectives of the Proverse Prize are: to encourage excellence and / or excellence and usefulness in publishable written work in the English Language, which can, in varying degrees, "delight and instruct". Entries are invited from anywhere in the world. Semi-finalists to date include writers born or resident in Andorra, Australia, Canada, Germany, Hong Kong, New Zealand, Nigeria, Singapore, South Africa, Taiwan, The Bahamas, the Peoples' Republic of China, the United Arab Emirates, the United Kingdom, the USA.

FOUNDERS: Verner Bickley and Gillian Bickley. To celebrate their lifelong love of words in all their forms as readers, writers, editors, academics, performers, and publishers.
HONORARY LEGAL ADVISOR: Mr Raymond T. L. Tse.
HONORARY ACCOUNTANT: Mr Neville Chow.
HONORARY JUDGES: Anonymous.
HONORARY ADVISORS: Bahamian poet Marion Bethel; UK translator, Margaret Clarke; UK linguist & lexicographer David Crystal; Canadian poet and academic, Jonathan Hart; Swedish linguist Björn Jernudd; Hong Kong University Librarian, Peter Sidorko; Singapore poet Edwin Thumboo; Czech novelist & poet Olga Walló.
HONORARY UK AGENT AND DISTRIBUTOR: Christine Penney
HONORARY ADMINISTRATORS: Proverse Hong Kong.

Proverse Prize Winners Whose Books Have Already Been Published By Proverse Hong Kong

Laura Solomon, Rebecca Jane Tomasis, Gillian Jones, David Diskin, Peter Gregoire, Sophronia Liu, Birgit Linder, James McCarthy, Celia Claase, Philip Chatting.

Summary Terms and Conditions
(for indication only & subject to revision)

The information below is for guidance only. Please refer to the year-specific Proverse Prize Entry Form & Terms & Conditions, which are uploaded in April each year onto the Proverse Hong Kong website: <www.proversepublishing.com>.

The free Proverse E-Newsletter includes ongoing information about the Proverse Prize. To be put on the E-Newsletter mailing-list, email: info@proversepublishing.com with your request.

The Prize
1) Publication by Proverse Hong Kong, with
2) Cash prize of HKD10,000 (HKD7.80 = approx. US$1.00)

Supplementary publication grants may be made to selected other entrants for publication by Proverse Hong Kong.

Depending on the quality of the work in any year, the prize may be shared by at most two entrants or withheld, as recommended by the judges.

In 2015, the entry fee was: HKD220.00 OR GBP32.00.

Writers are eligible, who are at least eighteen on the date they sign The Proverse Prize entry documents. There is no nationality or residence restriction.

Each submitted work must be an unpublished publishable single-author work of non-fiction, fiction or poetry, the original work of the entrant, and submitted in the English language. School textbooks and plays are ineligible.

Translated work: If the work entered is a translation from a language other than English, both the original work and the translation should be previously unpublished. The submitted work will not be judged as a translation but as an original work.

Extent of the Manuscript: within the range of what is usual for the genre of the work submitted. However, it is advisable that novellas be in the range 30,000 to 45,000 words); other fiction (e.g. novels, short-story collections) and non-fiction (e.g. autobiographies, biographies, diaries, letters, memoirs, essay collections, etc.) should be in the range, 75,000 to 100,000 words. Poetry collections / Poetry should be in the range, 5,000 to 25,000 words. Other word-counts and mixed-genre submissions are not ruled out.

Writers may choose, if they wish, to obtain the services of an Editor in presenting their work, and should acknowledge this help and the nature and extent of this help in the Entry Form.

KEY DATES FOR THE PROVERSE PRIZE IN ANY YEAR
(subject to confirmation and/or change)

Receipt of Entry Fees / Entry Documents	14 April to 31 May of the year of entry
Receipt of entered manuscripts	1 May to 30 June of the year of entry
Announcement of semi-finalists	July-September of the year of entry
Announcement of finalists	October-December of the year of entry
Announcement of winner/ max two winners (sharing the cash prize)	December of the year of entry to April of the year that follows the year of entry
Cash Award made	At the same time as publication of the work(s) adjudged the winner / joint-winners of the Proverse Prize
Publication of winning work(s)	In or after November of the year that follows the year of entry

NON-FICTION (INCLUDING BIOGRAPHY)
Published by Proverse Hong Kong

The Chinese of Macau a decade after the handover, by Jean Berlie. HK & UK, November 2012. Pbk. c.248pp. with 8pp. colour illustrations.
ISBN-13: 978-988-8167-37-1.

The complete court cases of Magistrate Frederick Stewart as reported in The China Mail, July 1881 to March 1882. Edited with commentary and chapters by Gillian Bickley. Essay by Dr Ian Grant. HK & UK, 2008. Preface by The Hon. Mr Justice Bokhary PJ, Court of Final Appeal. CD. 761pp. inc. notes. Supported by the Council of the Lord Wilson Heritage Trust.
ISBN-13: 978-988-17724-1-1

The development of education in Hong Kong, 1841-1897: as revealed by the early Education Reports of the Hong Kong Government, 1848-1896. Ed. Gillian Bickley. HK & UK, 2002. Hbk. 633pp., inc. bibliography. Supported by the Council of the Lord Wilson Heritage Trust.
ISBN-10: 962-85570-1-7; ISBN-13: 978-962-85570-1-1.

The diplomat of Kashgar: A Very Special Agent. The Life of Sir George Macartney, 18 January 1867 to 19 May 1945, by James McCarthy. HK & UK, 2014. ISBN 13: 978-988-8227-62-4.

Forward to Beijing! a guide to the Summer Olympics, by Verner Bickley. HK & UK, 2008. Message by Timothy Fok. Preface by The Hon. Dr Arnaldo de Oliveira Sales. With an essay, "A big idea" by Chris Wardlaw. Pbk. 260pp. with 16 b/w photographs.
ISBN-13: 978-988-99668-3-6.

The Golden Needle: the biography of Frederick Stewart (1836-1889), by Gillian Bickley. David C. Lam Institute for East-West Studies, Hong Kong Baptist University. HK & UK, 1997. Foreword by Lady Saltoun. Introduction by Sir David Wilson (now Lord Wilson). Pbk. 308pp., inc. bibliography, archival photographs.
ISBN-1: 962-8027-08-5; ISBN-13 978-962-8027-08-8.

The Golden Needle: the biography of Frederick Stewart (1836-1889). Full audio version on 14 CDs. Read by Verner Bickley.
ISBN: CD-962-8027-08-5;ISRC: HK-D94-00-00001-40.

Also, Teachers' and students' guide to the book and audio book, 'The Golden Needle: the biography of Frederick Stewart (1836-1889)'. Proverse Hong Kong Study Guides.
E-book. ISBN-10: 962-85570-9-2; ISBN-13: 978-962-85570-9-7. 24Reader e-book edition (2010), ISBN-13: 978-988-19320-5-1.

A magistrate's court in nineteenth century Hong Kong: Court in Time. Contributing Editor, Gillian Bickley. Contributors: Garry Tallentire, Geoffrey Roper, Timothy Hamlett, Christopher Coghlan, Verner Bickley. Preface by Sir T. L. Yang. 1st edn. HK & UK, 2005. Pbk. 531pp. inc. bibliography, notes, archival illustrations.
ISBN-10: 962-85570-4-1; ISBN-13: 978-962-85570-4-2.

A magistrate's court in nineteenth century Hong Kong, with additional discussion of "The Opium Ordinance": Court in Time. 2nd edn. HK & UK, 2009. Pbk. 536pp. inc. bibliography, notes, archival illustrations. ISBN-13: 978-988-17724-5-9.

Searching for Frederick and adventures along the way, by Verner Bickley. Hong Kong, 2001. Pbk. 420pp. Supported by the Hong Kong Arts Development Council. ISBN-10: 962-8783-20-3; ISBN-13: 978-962-8783-20-5.

The Stewarts of Bourtreebush, by Gillian Bickley. Aberdeen, UK, Centre for Scottish Studies, University of Aberdeen, 2003. Pbk. 153pp. Extensive documentation of the Scottish family of Frederick Stewart, founder of Hong Kong Government Education.
ISBN-10: 0-906265-34-7; ISBN-13: 978-0-906265-34-5.

AUTOBIOGRAPHY, MEMOIRS, LETTERS, DIARIES, TRAVEL
Published by Proverse Hong Kong

Chocolate's brown study in the bag, by Rupert Kwan Yun Chan. HK & UK, March 2011. Pbk. 112pp. + 16 colour pp. illustrations. Proverse Prize Finalist (2009).
ISBN: 978-988-19932-1-2.

Gin's tonic: ocean voyage, inner journey, by Virginia MacRobert. HK & UK, 2010. Preface by Ed Vaughan. Pbk. 600pp., inc. index, illustrations: colour photographs, author portrait. Supported by Hong Kong Arts Development Council.
ISBN-13: 978-988-17724-3-5.

In time of war, by Richard Collingwood-Selby. HK & UK, 2013. ISBN-13: 978-988-8167-36-4. Supported by Lord Wilson Heritage Trust.

A personal journey through sketching: the sketcher's art, by Errol Patrick Hugh. HK & UK, 2009. Introduction by Li Shiqiao. Hbk. 96pp. inc. 100+ original sketches and photographs by the author & author's portrait. 300mm x 215mm x 14mm. w. CD-ROM. ISBN-13: 978-988-18479-1-1.

Semper fi! The story of a vietnam era marine, by Orville Leverne Clubb. HK & UK, 2012. Pbk. 216pp. + 6pp photographs, sketch-map, inc. glossary.
ISBN-13: 978-988-19933-4-2.

Steps to Paradise and Beyond: Hawaii to China, Saudi Arabia, Hong Kong and Elsewhere, by Verner Bickley. HK & UK, 2013. Pbk. 480pp. + photographs, facsimiles.
Preface by Charles E. Morrison, President, East-West Center, Hawaii. Supported by Hong Kong Arts Development Council.
ISBN 13: 978-988-8167-40-1

Wannabe backpackers: the Latin American & Kenyan journey of five spoiled teenagers, by Gerald Yeung. HK & UK, 2009. Pbk. 164pp. inc. several b/w pix.
ISBN 978-988-17724-2-8.

NON-FICTION – CHINESE LANGUAGE

The Golden Needle: the biography of Frederick Stewart (1836-1889): Selections《香港開埠時的雙語教育——史釗域和母語教學》by Gillian Bickley. Translated by Hong-Lok Kwok. 2010. E-book. ISBN-13: 978-988-18905-4-2.

GENRES

Proverse publishes novels, novellas, short story collections and poetry collections; non-fiction including autobiography, biography, children's illustrated books, educational books, Hong Kong educational and legal history, memoirs, teenage / young adult books, and travel. Other genres may be added.

FIND OUT MORE ABOUT OUR AUTHORS BOOKS AND EVENTS

Visit our website
http://www.proversepublishing.com

Visit our distributor's website
<www.chineseupress.com>

Follow us on Twitter
Follow news and conversation: <twitter.com/Proversebooks>
OR
Copy and paste the following to your browser window and follow the instructions: https://twitter.com/#!/ProverseBooks

'Like us' on Facebook: www.facebook.com/ProversePress

Request our E-Newsletter
Send your request to info@proversepublishing.com.

Availability
Most titles are available in Hong Kong and world-wide from our Hong Kong based Distributor,
The Chinese University Press of Hong Kong,
The Chinese University of Hong Kong, Shatin, NT,
Hong Kong SAR, China. Web: chineseupress.com

All titles are available from Proverse Hong Kong and the Proverse Hong Kong UK-based Distributor.

We have stock-holding retailers in Hong Kong,
Singapore (Select Books),
Canada (Elizabeth Campbell Books),
Principality of Andorra (Llibreria La Puça, La Llibreria).

Orders can be made from bookshops in the UK and elsewhere.

Ebooks
Most of our titles are available also as Ebooks.

Printed in Great Britain
by Amazon